"I've known Bob for years, and I've seen his style of leadership in action. It works. I recommend this book to you." —**Dr. Arthur Laffer**, Laffer Associates, former member of President Reagan's Economic Policy Advisory Board and named in *The Wall Street Journal*'s Gallery of the Greatest People Who Influence Our Daily Business

*　*　*

"Bob Bailey distinguishes between managing and leading and provides succinct, usable guidelines to help good managers become good leaders." —**Joe Sheldrick**, Publisher, Battelle Press

*　*　*

"On more than one occasion, I've come across a business book that is so much on target of sound management and State Auto's culture that I've recommended it to our associates. Bob Bailey's **PLAIN TALK ABOUT LEADERSHIP** is a book that fits this 'must read' definition. It is particularly meaningful to those of us who have spent most of our working lives seeing how the common sense principles that Bob espouses can make a monumental difference in a company's performance.

"It is a fast-paced book, but one that should not be read once and placed on the shelf. Its true value can only be manifested by doing what I did with my copy—place a series of little sticky notes with a description of the topic of your favorite chapters, then leave it within easy access of your chair. You'll find that you will reach for it often. And you will find the advice will make you a more effective and respected leader, in your company and in your community." —**Robert H. Moone**, Chairman of the Board, President and Chief Executive Officer, State Auto Insurance Companies

PLAIN TALK ABOUT
LEADERSHIP
SILVER BULLETS FOR SUCCESS

Robert L. Bailey

Franklin University Press

Library of Congress Cataloging-in-Publications Data

Bailey, Robert L., 1933–
    Plain talk about leadership : silver bullets for success /
Robert L. Bailey
        p. cm.
        Includes index.
        LCCN: 2001131753
        ISBN: 1-931604-01-0

    1. Leadership.   I. Title

HD57.7.B35 2002   658.4'092
                             QBI01-201301

Printed in the United States of America

Copyright © 2002 Franklin University Press

Franklin University Press
201 South Grant Avenue
Columbus, Ohio 43215-5399
614-744-3040
E-mail: mcclells@franklin.edu
www.franklin.edu

DEDICATION

To my wife, Sylvia, who has put up with me for 45 years despite my unbelievably long work hours, hectic travel schedule, and a tendency toward workaholism. She always fixed my breakfast, no matter at what hour I arose to catch an early morning flight. When I decided that it would be quiet, peaceful, and fun if we lived on a farm, she agreed to the move—not because *she* wanted to but because *I* wanted to. She has continued to act as if it is "fun" even when someone stops in the middle of the night to tell us that our cattle are out on the public road. "Was this in the marriage contract?" she asks.

She managed to raise successfully three wonderful children—Janet, Nancy and Jim. She didn't do it entirely alone, but she contributed more to the process than I did. Today, they are all successful young adults with an excellent work ethic and values that the most critical would admire. No parent could feel more fortunate. Now they are raising their own children—Jenny, Justin, Megan, Zack, and Cody—undoubtedly the finest grandchildren in the universe. You would expect such bias from a grandfather.

"We'll have more time to be together after your retirement," Sylvia often said. But it hasn't yet worked out that way. My schedule remains hectic. Frankly, I wasn't certain that I could exist peacefully without involvement with the insurance company of which I was president, chairman, and CEO for many years. I love the company and I love its people like members of my family. They are the folks who taught me what I know about leadership and tolerated me when I made management mistakes. They seemed to be saying, "OK, try it again and see if you can get it right this time."

Today, I have a combination of activities that add up to significantly more than a full-time job: writer and public speaker; farmer, cattleman, horseman; and breeder of miniature donkeys. I'm fully committed to the idea that early retirement applies to those who quit before they die.

Sylvia said she would never marry a farmer, and I assured her back in 1956 that being reared on a Kansas farm was all I ever wanted of that. But by now we have figured it out: farming *can* be fun for those who don't have to do it.

Through all this "career change," Sylvia has been as supportive as she was of my "day job" for more than forty years. She even admits—on occasion—that these so-called retirement years are the most productive, fulfilling, and happy years of our lives.

No one could be more fortunate in having a loving, supportive wife and family. I extend to them my thanks for tolerating me for all these years—to my children specifically for leading such exemplary lives for their own children.

R.L.B.

ABOUT THE AUTHOR

It is fitting that Bob Bailey, a member of the Franklin University Board of Trustees and a long time personal friend and mentor, would author the first book on leadership published by the Franklin University Press. Bob teaches leadership in our unique Organizational Leadership (undergraduate) major, and at the same time distinguishes himself as a "real world" business leader.

How do I, as a friend and disciple, introduce him to you? The easiest way is to urge you to read this book. In its pages you will get to know Bob Bailey. You will meet a leader who truly leads by example, and his examples are presented in the "plain talk" style that is characteristically Bob Bailey. You may feel you are sitting in a comfortable chair (and you might be) learning leadership in a straightforward manner, without frills, or verbiage.

Bob's writing style is like his leadership, based on stories (examples) of how things work. As you read, you will develop a unique rapport with Bob, as if you were in the same room listening to him. How do I know that? Because I have been there. As I read his words, I can't help but think of my own examples of how his plain talk works in everyday leadership.

But how do I get you to read his book? Perhaps by assuring you that his *Silver Bullets for Success* work. How do I do that? By examining Bob's successes, professional and personal. His professional success centers on his role at State Auto Insurance Companies, complemented by his leadership in the insurance industry.

Bob Bailey retired from State Auto Insurance Companies on December 31, 2000, after 27 years of wanting to come to work everyday. He retired not because he wanted to, but because, in his own words, he "couldn't know what he knows today and still be 42 years old." Since his retirement at a "young" 67 years of age, he has been devoting his time to writing and public speaking on leadership, selling value (his next book), and trends in the property/casualty insurance industry.

Under his leadership of State Auto since 1983, several companies were added to the State Auto Group—now 12 insurance companies and several other subsidiaries. Bob took those companies into 13 additional states (now 27 in total), and he was the mastermind behind taking the companies public in 1991 with the formation of State Auto Financial Corporation (STFC).

This new, publicly owned company has produced an enviable record. Since STFC's first full year as a public corporation through Bob's retirement in 2000, compound average growth rates were: revenues 14%; earnings per share 23%; equity 14%; assets 17%; and book value per share 16%. From 1991 through 1997, State Auto stock was the 85th best performer on the NASDAQ exchange. In October 2000, *Investor's Business Daily* listed State Auto as one of the 25 best insurance companies in the United States.

With the four acquisitions that were brought about under his leadership, sales rose from $214 million to more than $1 billion, and net worth increased from $139 million to $900 million. Simply put, State Auto Insurance Companies has become one of the top performing property/casualty insurance organizations in our country. Service levels improved drastically under what he calls an "overwhelming service" objective.

At the same time, employee morale reached the highest level ever (I know, I have seen it!), thanks to Bob's strong focus on communication (communication, communication), recognition, and motivation. The accomplishments under Bob's leadership have been noted by Tom Peters in his best selling books on business management.

It all began when Bob entered the insurance business in 1958 with Western Casualty and Surety Company of Fort Scott, Kansas, now a part of the Safeco Insurance Group. He is a graduate of Fort Scott Community College (alumnus of the year) and Pittsburg (the one in Kansas) State University. He holds the Chartered Property and Casualty (CPCU) and Associate in Risk Management designations. As you would expect of such a leader, he has served on numerous insurance-industry and community (including Franklin's) boards.

A professional success? Surely! But what about this leader as a family man? He has been married to Sylvia for over 45 years and together they have raised three wonderful children and have the finest grandchildren in the universe (Bob's words). And after all of this, he has returned to the farm to raise horses, cattle, and miniature donkeys. A personal success? You bet!

Another friend of mine once said, "a person should look forward to going to work in the morning and coming home at night." Bob Bailey has been doing both for over 40 years. Along the way, he has been writing his philosophy for leadership.

Now that you have been properly introduced to Bob, enjoy his plain-talk writings, learn from him (as so many of us already have), and create your own successes through his silver bullets!

—PAUL OTTE
President, Franklin University

CONTENTS

Section III
LEARNING HOW TO COMMUNICATE

Section IV
GET READY, GET SET, COMMUNICATE

Section V
WHAT ABOUT ME?

Section VI
THE MAGIC OF MOTIVATION

Section VII
BUILDING THE TEAM

Section VIII
A PENNY SAVED

Section IX
SERVING CUSTOMERS

FOREWORD

In the books I have written in the past decade with Don Peppers, we have focused on the development and deployment of a new strategy for competing in the post-industrial age. Variously called 1to1 Customer Relationship Management or "Learning Relationships," the theory focuses an organization on its customers and the equity of the customer base. One-to-one, in practice, requires establishment of a special relationship with each customer, one customer at a time.

It has been called a revolutionary theory, but it is the inevitable result of key technological innovations.

The book you hold in your hands, Bob Bailey's *Plain Talk About Leadership: Silver Bullets for Success*, serves to remind us that there are fundamental truths and time-tested principles that must be the foundation of a strong relationship, regardless of technological innovation. Compassion, integrity, loyalty, and dedication to a task are the critical cornerstones, mixed with common sense and a passion to serve others.

Bailey's book is the natural complement to new thinking about building customer relationships. Fact is, for a relationship to begin or to continue, all parties have to agree to its existence. This book persuasively makes the point that any relationship—if it is going to grow and have meaning—must be intensely personal and be characterized by feelings of respect and trust that are mutual and reciprocal.

These are the qualities that must precede and provide a context for a series of collaborative interactions.

Adherence to these principles, described in Bailey's stories and summarized as *"silver bullets,"* enhances a business because they cause customers to say, "Not only do you know and remember me, you *care* about me!"

In *The One to One Manager: Real-World Lessons in Customer Relationship Management* (1999), we cited examples from Amazon.com, British Airways, and other organizations where customers feel trusted, respected, and valued as a result of services provided to them. Amazon.com and British Airways become "preferred" because they are seen as organizations that have sincere concern for the customer's welfare.

Without using the language that characterizes customer-centric practices, Bailey nevertheless emphasizes the same core concept— the individual *really* matters, and businesses will not achieve sustainable market advantage until they make the organizational changes necessary to achieve the objective of building a company that manages individual relationships.

If you are a manager charged with the responsibility of maximizing the potential of those with whom you work, this book is a "must read." It contains a vast amount of wisdom from a very smart guy who boasts a successful career and a lifetime of learning. It's presented in a way that makes you feel that Bob Bailey is in your living room and the two of you are having a conversation about a variety of topics that are critical to the success of your organization.

Listen carefully. This is wisdom founded in values from the past, applied to the future. Your future, and the future of your company

—MARTHA ROGERS, PH.D.

EXECUTIVE SUMMARY

I know—it is highly unusual to start a book with an Executive Summary. It just proves, I suppose, that I'm a fugitive from the corporate world, where busy executives want to be informed fast. So, what's leadership all about? Find the answer here—in a couple of pages.

Try this exercise with a line up of a few associates or members of your family. Have them count off—1, 2, 1, 2, 1, 2, etc. Then ask each number one to place the palm of his or her right hand against the palm of the right hand of the neighboring number two. Now ask the number ones to push as hard as they can.

What happened? If the participants complied with your instructions, the number ones pushed and the number twos yielded. However, in all likelihood, the number twos pushed back. It is inherent in humans to resist when they are pushed. You don't like to be pushed—I don't like to be pushed, either.

That's the first lesson. *Management*, in general, has come to connote a pushing process, while management by *leadership* implies a process through which employees follow willingly.

Certainly leadership is more complicated than that; leadership has many dimensions. But I can offer one word that most closely sums up all those dimensions. That word is *communication*. Great leaders tend to be great communicators. And one word best sums up communication. That word is *example*. No matter what is said, no matter what is written, no matter how talented is the company's public relations staff, a message is not effective unless the leader sets an appropriate example.

So, here's the quick and dirty essence of management by leadership. Don't push; communicate; and set a positive example.

That sounds simple, but it really isn't. Communicating is a difficult process. Setting a positive example is even tougher. That is why it's easy to get ahead in management in most companies—there is little competition. Most people are not willing to pay the price. No book or class or seminar can shortcut the process. A manager or supervisor must apply to the process a high level of energy, commitment, and sacrifice.

For managers and aspiring managers who have heard everything they ever want to hear about becoming an effective leader, I have this suggestion. Route this book to the most promising young executive in your company. Ask him or her to read it and then let you know if there is anything new in it worth knowing. I promise you'll be told that you missed a lot of good stuff.

SILVER BULLETS

▲ Management generally implies a pushing process. Management by leadership does not.

▲ The best word to sum up all the dimensions of leadership is communication. Great leaders tend to be great communicators.

▲ The best word to sum up communication is *example*. It doesn't matter what is said or written. It's what the leader *does* that counts most.

SECTION I
Introduction

1

THERE IS NO BEANIE BABY MANAGEMENT

Each year there's a new rage in children's toys—Cabbage Patch dolls, Beanie Babies, Pokémon cards. I can't remember many of the others, and chances are the kids can't remember them either—even though, at the time, they thought they would be considered underprivileged without them.

So it is with management fads. Each year, a new one appears, touted by its advocates as the salvation of the free enterprise system. A few months later most of us can't even remember its name.

Why aren't these techniques indelibly inscribed on the brain of every successful manager? Because management is a long-term learning process. Because there are no silver bullets (except, of course, those that summarize each chapter of this book). There are no short cuts. Management people pick up a little here and a little there, and during the course of a career some of them become successful, effective leaders.

Management is like parenting. Parents read, study, observe, and experiment. Throughout the course of their careers as parents—the most important management/leadership job any of us will ever have—they create a system, a style, a series of parenting techniques. What worked for one child may not work for the second. And what worked for the second may not work for the third. By the time the youngest child graduates from college, gets married, and moves away from home, the parents are convinced that they've got it. They tend to learn how to be good parents at a point in their lives when they don't need to know.

It would be a severe overstatement (if not an out-and-out lie) to say that I've got this thing called leadership down pat. Yes, I've made progress, but I'm still learning every day. I still have a lot to learn, even though "the kids have moved away."

The inspiration for this book came from efforts to perpetuate the management philosophy of the company of which I was president, chairman, and CEO for many years. As my retirement drew near and we began the transition process, I promised the Board of Directors and the stockholders that I would be available to give advice and counsel whenever necessary (as it turned out, I gave it when *unnecessary*, too). I found myself repeating to my successor and other senior managers some of the management lessons we had learned over the years. These were lessons learned by reading virtually every worthwhile management book that came along (as well as many that were not worthwhile), by reading biographies and autobiographies of successful business people, by attending management meetings and seminars, by observing other managers both good and bad (more bad than good), and by grinding it out the hard way—managing people and making mistakes.

Eventually, I thought it might be helpful to write down some of those management lessons—some of the things that I believed would help assure the continued success of our company. So I started to write on my faithful laptop, generally on the tray table of an airplane or sitting in the concourse of a noisy airport.

Finally, it occurred to me that these lessons might be helpful to a broader audience of managers and aspiring managers who are trying to perfect the art of leadership. Thus, this book was born.

When I was asked why I wanted to give management advice to our competitors, I was reminded of Ira Hayes, a former sales executive with NCR. Ira conducted outstanding sales seminars throughout the country. I heard Ira several times and I always went home with several pages of excellent sales tips. At one seminar someone asked, "Mr. Hayes, why do you go around the country telling your competitors how to compete with you?" Without hesitation he answered, "Hell, our own people won't even do it."

Most people who read this book will find good ideas that they fully intend to put to work. But most won't follow through. Why? Because the process of good management (i.e., leadership) requires more hard work, commitment, and sacrifice than most are willing to give. I didn't tell you that this was going to be easy.

Generally speaking, two types of people benefit from reading books like this one: those who manage companies in trouble and are looking for ways to dig out of the hole and those who have the seeds of leadership and are looking for ways to improve their skills.

I said earlier that it is easy to get ahead in management in most American companies. Corporate America is screaming for management people who can get results. While your competitors are coasting along taking advantage of every perk within reach, you can start sharpening your leadership skills this very day.

But, again, it's hard work. That's why senior management positions normally pay substantial sums of money. And good managers are worth every penny they get. The emphasis, however, is on *results*. I too am offended by the high salaries and bonuses of top executives whose companies are failing—companies that were able to continue in existence only through "restructuring" and layoffs of hundreds or thousands of employees. When I see mass layoffs of people, I ask, "I wonder who hired them?" What a horrible way to treat people! How to deal with over-staffing problems is one of the things you will learn in this book.

Are you ready? Start today by adopting one new leadership technique that will help you and your company become more successful.

SILVER BULLETS

▲ Leadership in management is an ongoing learning process.

▲ Successful managers learn a little here and a little there.

▲ Leadership in management involves hard work, commitment, and sacrifice. There are no short cuts.

▲ It's easy to get ahead in management. There is little competition. Most people are not willing to pay the price.

2
WHEN THE CAT'S AWAY

What does it mean to be a manager?

Not long ago I reviewed the structure of a small company with about 27 employees. Twelve, about 44%, held management jobs. Those 12 earned about 65% of the total payroll.

Something is wrong with that picture. One of the great truths that history has taught us— one that we've been trying to disprove for hundreds of years—is that in any effective organization, most of the people must perform activities that produce goods or services—the activities that bring in the income, pay the bills, produce a profit.

Although it may be a disappointment to some people and some will disagree strenuously, management isn't one of those activities. Don't get me wrong. Management is necessary, but the process known as management is an overhead cost.

The first step in making any organization successful is to determine a proper role for management and the extent to which management is necessary. Start by administering the *When the Cat's Away* test.

What effect would it have on the company (or department or unit within the company) if the manager were to be away for one day? Would progress stop? Would customers be served? Would the company be adversely affected in some way?

Not many people would even notice. Some might even say that everything went smoother than normal because the boss wasn't around to mess things up.

What about a two-day absence? A week? Up to now I haven't found a company that couldn't get along pretty well when someone takes a week off.

Two weeks? A month? Is the same true?

Or six months?

At some point the answer may get fuzzy, but even at six months it's probably not a slam-dunk.

Throughout history, we've had great leaders. Charlemagne, king of the Franks and emperor of the Roman Empire, was one of them. He was so revered as a leader that when he died in 814 his body was embalmed, dressed in royal robes, topped off with the crown, and propped up for all to see until his burial in 1215. Meanwhile, the empire survived quite well. Yes, that's an extreme example, but perhaps it adds a perspective of humility for those of us who have been assigned leadership roles.

A recent newspaper article reported a major corporation's elimination of some 700 jobs, most in the *middle management* ranks. Stories like that are not uncommon. They're in the newspapers nearly every day. But there's more to the story. Some six months after the layoffs, the CEO said his company was doing well without those 700 people. "As a matter of fact," he continued, "things are going so well that we can't figure out what any of them had been doing." King Charlemagne lives.

It's safe to say that nobody in the company had authorized the hiring of 700 middle management people they didn't think they needed. And had any of the 700 people been asked if he or she were working hard—and contributing to the goals of the corporation—undoubtedly the answer would have been "yes."

In any study of the field of management—and the segment of management called *leadership*—the first questions must be: Why does management exist? How many managers—or how few—are really necessary? Although this is far from a scientific survey, it's been my observation that most companies have too many people with manager titles, not too few.

Also, as a long-time observer of human nature and of successful and unsuccessful companies, I'm totally convinced that most problems are management problems; that poor management is worse than no management; and that too much management is worse than too little management.

SILVER BULLETS

▲ Management is overhead. Most of the work force must work—to produce the goods and services for which customers pay.

▲ Is the management position truly necessary? How many—or how few—managers are really required? Most companies have too many managers, not too few.

▲ Most business problems are management problems. Poor management is worse than no management. Too much management is worse than too little management.

3
WHY THE BIG BUCKS?

Managers, for the most part, make significantly more money than *doers*—the rank and file workers in a company. Therefore, if the forces of economics are working as they should, those who hold *management* jobs should be adding significant value to the company.

Yet it's unlikely that management people know more about any given job in the company than others do. In my company, accountants know more about accounting than I do; computer programmers can program better than I can (history's greatest understatement); underwriters can underwrite better than I can; claim representatives can settle claims better than I can; data entry operators can enter data into the computer faster and more accurately than I can. The list encompasses virtually every activity in our company.

If employees can do most activities better than the manager, why is the manager worth the big bucks? What value is added by the manager? I believe there are three specific elements in the way a good manager adds value:

He or she gets defined, desired results

. . . by working through people

. . . within a defined philosophical framework.

Getting *defined, desired results* requires that the objectives be specific, that they be written down, and that they be measurable. Same day customer service, for example. Or perhaps a return on equity of 15%; a sales increase of 20%; meeting defined quality standards 100% of the time. I believe every job is measurable, including the job of cleaning rest rooms. Many people have taken exception with me on this point, but I've yet to see a job that can't be measured. A small group of people brainstorming for a while will always come up with a workable answer.

Whatever the department or unit is supposed to do, the manager should be able to define it, measure it, and have the means at hand to accomplish it. If the manager doesn't have the resources to do the job, there will be finger pointing—"I couldn't do my job because . . . ."

Through people means that the manager utilizes people to get those desired, defined results. A person who doesn't utilize people to get the job done is not a manager. I don't accept the idea that people can hold manager titles because they manage functions and not people. Although there may be some merit to the proposition that throwing manager titles around is cheaper than giving salary increases, I still don't like the idea.

Working *within a defined philosophical framework* is harder to explain—and harder to accomplish, but, in my view, it's the most important dimension of the management process. It involves the treatment of all the constituencies served by the company— customers, sales people, employees, investors. It involves the company's role in the community and in its industry. It can be a negative framework—"This company will do anything to make a profit and we don't care how you do it!"—or it can be a positive framework. One can *manage* within a negative philosophical framework, but most people will not follow a leader who operates within such a philosophical framework.

At our company the philosophical framework is that we *always do the right thing*. And we do the right thing regardless of what the contract says and regardless of what we might be able to get away with. At first blush one might think that *doing the right thing* is not definable, but I've found that that's not the case. If you hire the right people, they know.

You can name companies in your community that have a reputation for treating people poorly. People say, "That's the last place I would ever want to work," or, "I would never do business there." On the other hand, there are companies that have little turnover and have no difficulty hiring new people, regardless of the employment market, because "it's a great place to work." In 1999, Southwest airlines had 6,000 job openings. Yet it received 170,000 applications for those 6,000 jobs—in an economy that had virtually no unemployment, when everybody who had a will to work was working. This is no accident. Southwest has a reputation of being a great place to work.

It's the role of the manager to create a philosophical framework that reflects the values of the company—a framework so clearly understood that people at all levels—from officers to the newest employee—know how to *do the right thing*.

Building such a culture can be difficult, depending on the starting point. Keeping it going once it's established is fairly simple, since the culture itself attracts people who believe as you do.

Ethics is a part of a philosophical framework. Much is written about ethics these days, and frankly I disagree with much of it. Too many people who consider themselves ethics experts relate ethics to profits. Some seem to have the impression that business is inherently bad—that profit is a dirty word. That simply is not the case.

Several years back, I attended a seminar on ethics conducted by the president of a theological seminary. If I understood his message, he said that Ray Kroc, the founder of McDonald's, was unethical because he employed people throughout the world at minimum wage levels and became wealthy in the process. He said that Sam Walton, founder of Wal-Mart, was likewise unethical because he continued to amass great wealth until the time of his death. The seminar leader did not seem to understand that thousands of jobs had been created by these individuals, many right here in our own community. Not only are there hundreds of thousands of employees of these companies, but also there are hundreds of thousands of jobs created by suppliers of services and products sold by these companies.

Profitable companies, and individuals who have created wealth, pay the preponderance of taxes to government. Most contributions to charities are made by profitable companies and wealthy individuals. Profitable companies and wealthy people do more than their fair share to help others. I can't imagine the conditions under which all of us would live if it were not possible to create wealth.

Our ethics test is simple: No one should be embarrassed if tomorrow morning his or her actions are outlined on the front page of *The Columbus Dispatch*, our local newspaper, or *USA Today*. If the majority of readers would read the account and say, "I think they did the right thing," that's the behavior we expect and encourage.

All this is included within a company's philosophical framework. It's the creation of a value system. It's what makes one company different from another in the same industry. It's built by people called managers. Managers who can do the job effectively are worth big bucks.

SILVER BULLETS

▲ A manager adds value by getting desired, defined results through people, and within a defined philosophical framework.

▲ Building the philosophical framework—how customers, sales people, employees and others are treated—and what role the company plays in its community and its industry are the hardest parts.

▲ Ethics is a part of the framework. No one should ever be embarrassed if the actions of the company are published in tomorrow's newspaper. Employees should understand how to *do the right thing*. This is what makes your company different from other companies in your industry.

The Big Picture

4

SURPRISE!

This book is about leadership. Yet so far I've talked about the big umbrella of *management* more than the single phase of management called *leadership*. Why?

This will be a surprise to many of you, but despite nearly everyone's interest in having a good leader—despite the efforts of those who claim to be good leaders—*I've never known a leader who is always followed*. OK, so you're not that surprised.

It's true, I believe, that nearly everyone wants a good leader. And certainly many claim to be good leaders. In the last campaign for the presidency of the United States, one candidate said, "I've learned to lead." Another said, "I'm more interested in leadership than polls or politics." Still another stated, "You deserve a leader." The media has reported that pronouncements of leadership were among the best applause lines of the campaign.

In politics, a 50% favorable rating is super. In business, a good leader should do much better than that. But there will still be employees who have their own agendas that are inconsistent with the direction of the employer; an employee may have a perform-ance problem that must be dealt with firmly; or an employee may not have the ability to perform, having been poorly selected in the first place. Under such circumstances, the *management* dimension must take over.

The field of management involves getting the desired results—through people—within the philosophical framework we discussed earlier. Leadership is only one technique used in management; some circumstances require other approaches.

Dishonesty is one such circumstance; it requires a tough stance. When a person cheats the company or a customer, the only option is termination. Zero tolerance.

Other circumstances require a "this is what you do—like it or not—and if you don't do it you're fired" approach. That's not leadership, but it's definitely management.

There are only a few situations in which "this is what you do—like it or not" form of management is acceptable. One is in the field of politics. In many cases a politician has been able to build a cadre of so-called *loyal followers* through threats of personal destruction if the employee makes any negative comment about the politician. This would never work in the free enterprise system today—and I don't fully understand why it works in politics. I asked one former employee of a U. S. Congressman why employees put up with this behavior, and he answered, "Power, prestige, perks, and chicks." I hope that's an exaggeration, but unfortunately, this behavior hap-pens in too many instances on both sides of the political fence.

Beyond politics, this style of management may also be appropriate when the situation is so critical that people expect firm, direct instruction. An extreme case is, "Fire! Get out of the building!" It's unlikely that anyone will say, "Who does that so-and-so think he is bossing me around like that." Managers brought in to turn around a failing company often must make fast, arbitrary decisions—and people will respond positively, knowing that the health and welfare of the company and all its people are at stake.

Finally, and most importantly, this style of management is appropriate when an employee has severe performance problems that the manager has been unable to solve by use of more acceptable leadership techniques. But this is a last resort. Before implementing the arbitrary "do it or else" management technique, look at other factors that may have influenced the employee's poor performance. Perhaps he or she is in the wrong job. It's usually worthwhile to try that person in another job requiring a different set of skills.

Most of us are not overwhelmingly successful as managers because we tend to have one style of management. And this one style does not fit every situation with every employee. Effective management normally requires a combination of leadership and management techniques.

SILVER BULLETS

▲ Leaders are not always followed.

▲ When employees do not follow, sometimes the management dimension must be added. Leadership is only one dimension of management.

▲ Certain circumstances require tough stances. Dishonesty, for instance. Termination is the only option—zero tolerance.

▲ The "this is what you do—like it or not" form of management may be appropriate in extreme situations, such as when survival of the company is at stake or when an employee has severe performance problems that have not been solved by using leadership techniques.

▲ Effective management requires a combination of leadership and management techniques.

5
THEN AND NOW

The qualities of leadership really haven't changed through the years. What has changed is the extent to which use of leadership is required.

Sixty years ago probably more than 90% of the techniques used to get results fell under the banner of "this is what you do" management rather than the banner of leadership. Proportionately the field of management looked like this.

In those days managers could be rather arbitrary and get away with it. People were so afraid of losing their jobs that they would put up with just about any form of bad behavior on the part of their bosses.

Today, the picture is different. The management field looks more like this:

Today, not many employees will take much guff from their bosses. The unemployment rate is so low that any reasonably good person (and probably most who are unreasonably bad) can get a dozen jobs before sunset tomorrow. Even the acts of terrorism in September 2001 are not likely to change the unemployment picture for long. Furthermore, literally dozens of safety nets are available—from unemployment insurance and other taxpayer-funded services, to services from charitable agencies. Basic help with food, clothing, and shelter are available to just about every-one, whether or not they are willing or able to work. Fear of los-ing a job is seldom a motivator in today's world.

If that's not good enough, most people are protected by law in some manner—age, sex, disability, religion, etc. A creative lawyer can probably figure out some way an employee can hit the jackpot by claiming discrimination by the employer.

In the future, chances are good that the management field will look more like this:

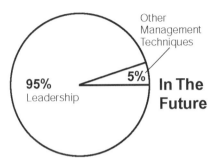

What could change this trend? Another 1929-style depression that brings about a serious unemployment situation? That is not likely because of the availability of all the safety nets. And, of course, an economic crisis like that is not likely to occur today. If I'm right, the manager of the future had better start polishing up his or her leadership techniques.

SILVER BULLETS

▲ Leadership hasn't changed through the years. What has changed is the extent to which leadership skills are required.

▲ During periods of dismal economic conditions, workers are afraid of losing their jobs, so they'll put up with bad behavior by their bosses.

▲ When economic times are good, many jobs are available else-where—and dozens of safety nets are available. Few have to worry about food, shelter and the basic necessities of life. Fear of losing a job is not a motivator.

▲ It appears likely that the manager of the future will have to polish his or her leadership skills.

Learning How to Communicate

6
A BIG-SHOT-FREE COMPANY

Remember, the word that best captures the essence of leadership is *communication*. And the activity that best lays the groundwork for all communication is: *Smile!* Try it! It doesn't hurt. And you might even find that you will feel a little better.

A smile is a universal language. It's performed the same way and has the same meaning throughout the world. Babies can do it when they are only a few weeks old. Then some of us spend the rest of our lives trying to learn *not* to smile—apparently so others can't penetrate our outer shell.

Smile . . . I know it's hard, but you can do it. I promise.

If a smile has not been a part of your work routine for many years, when you do start to smile people will probably say, "I wonder what's wrong with him?" or "I wonder what she wants of me?" It will take weeks or months to overcome the suspicious nature of your people—but ultimately they'll get to know the new you. They'll like the new you. And you'll like the new you.

When they like the new you and trust the new you, the door will begin to open for good, sound, two-way communication.

Next, speak to the people you meet in the hallway throughout the day. Everybody has a name, and it's the most pleasant sounding word to anyone in any language. If you don't know a person's name just say "Good morning" or "Good afternoon" anyway. Learn one new name a day. Over the course of a year you'll learn the names of quite a few of your people. In a 20-year career, you'll know practically everybody.

A long-time employee of a major local corporation commented to me about the company's new CEO: "He never speaks to anyone and many of the employees are talking about it." Sure, a new CEO has a lot of things to be thinking about, but a smile and a simple *good morning* or *good afternoon* shouldn't add to the CEO's burdens and in fact could go a long way toward building a team spirit that could remove some of the burdens he is carrying.

Call your customers by name. Through the years, our family purchased gasoline for several of our cars at a nearby gas station. Even though we were great customers—because we burned a lot of gasoline—nobody ever called any of us by name, even though our name was obvious because we used credit cards most of the time. This didn't sink in until I had a driving trip to Nashville, Tennessee. I stopped to fill up and paid with a credit card. The attendant said, "Mr. Bailey, thank you for stopping at" (and he named his station). "Please stop again the next time you're in Nashville." I can't remember the name of the station, but I do remember its location and have stopped there several times since.

I was so impressed with those folks—where I had never done business before—that I never again bought gasoline at the other station. Failing to call me by name cost them a lot of money over the years.

If you really want to lock in customers, call them by name.

"But I'm not good with names," you'll probably say. Most of us aren't. Still, if you will concentrate on one person and one name each day, you'll find that your name-remembering skills will improve.

Call employees by their first names. And encourage them to call you by your first name. You will lose no respect as a leader by using first names and communicating with your people on their level.

This sounds so simple that it may appear laughable. Yet in dozens of companies I have visited, I find myself smiling and speaking to people I have never seen before—will probably never see again—while the company's CEO who is with me seems to "walk through" the same individuals as if they weren't there.

Smile and speak. These are the first important steps to creating a Big-Shot-Free Company. In the most successful organizations I know, there is an absence of big shots. Big shots tend to stifle communication.

The Big-Shot-Free Company is run by a person who eats in the company cafeteria or lunchroom alongside everyone else. Sometimes I call the cafeteria the *Communications Center,* for communication is more likely to take place there than any other place in the company. Employees communicate with other employees, including employees in other departments. It's an opportunity for management people to communicate with employees at every level.

Yes, there have been times when I paralyzed a conversation in mid-syllable when I sat down at a cafeteria table, but over time employees got used to it. Then someone would say, "Did you know that such and such is causing a service breakdown in Department X?" Or, "I think we can save Y% of our time if we changed this procedure." When employees learn that you welcome their comments (and, yes, that takes a while) and when they learn that they will not get into trouble with their immediate superiors by giving you their suggestions, employees learn quickly that it's OK to tell you what's on their minds.

Of course, you must follow-up on those suggestions. If they see no action, they'll think you don't really care. If you appear not to care, they'll not bother to give you their suggestions.

Paul Otte, the President of Franklin University and a long-time friend, tells me that our company is one of the few that he visits that passes his *Cafeteria Test*. In most companies, Paul tells me he sees employees in the cafeteria reading the newspaper or watching the big screen TV. "In your cafeteria," Paul says, "your people are smiling and visiting with one another. They obviously like one another and like working there."

Smile. Say "good morning." Make certain that there are no big shots around.

Incidentally, when making an investment in the stock market, I like companies that are headed by non-big shots. They tend to be hands-on managers who know what's going on in their companies. And chances are they produce better results through the years.

These are the critical first steps in learning to communicate and creating an environment in which communication is easy.

SILVER BULLETS

▲ A *smile* lays the groundwork for all communication.

▲ When employees like you and trust you, the door opens for effective two-way communication.

▲ Speak to your people. Call them by their first names. And encourage them to call you by your first name.

▲ Create a Big-Shot-Free Company. Eat in the company cafeteria or lunchroom like everyone else. Big shots tend to stifle communication.

7

WHY MOST LEADERS FAIL

Now, for the really hard part. One dimension of effective communication is so powerful that without it most efforts to communicate fail. The lack of this dimension is the reason most leaders fail. That critical dimension is *example*.

Most parents understand the significance of this aspect of communication. Not long ago my wife and I were seated in the non-smoking section of a restaurant. In the smoking section (annoyingly right across the aisle) was seated a young mother probably in her early 30s with a little girl, probably four or five years old. "Don't smoke these things," the mother advised the little girl, "they're not good for you." What message was she communicating as she puffed away on her cigarette? Don't smoke, because that's what I said? Or do smoke, because that's what I'm doing?

My wife knows a lady who has two young daughters, one in junior high and one in high school, and mom doesn't want her daughters to know that she smokes. "Therefore," she says with pride, "when I'm at home, I smoke only in the bathroom." First, who does she think she's kidding? Generally we know who the smokers are, even among the strangers on an elevator with us. Second, what message is being communicated—it's OK to smoke as long as you sneak around doing it?

Most of us understand the power of example in our personal lives, but somehow we overlook its importance at the corporate level. Frankly, it's even more important—and even more powerful—in a company leadership role because, where a larger number of people are involved, communication must be consistent. Every possible means must be used to send the same positive message to all the people. There is no room for exceptions or fuzzy messages.

A short story:

The CEO has communicated widely with all the employees the importance of reducing expenses if the company is to compete profitably in the marketplace, grow and prosper, and provide opportunities and security for its people. All forms of internal communication have been used—written, spoken, intranet—with the message created by a talented group of specialists who use the English language with skill and precision.

During the course of the communication campaign, the company helicopter lands on the company lawn on a Wednesday afternoon. As the windows shake from the blast of the helicopter blades, the employees look out the window at several executives boarding the helicopter, golf clubs in tow. Perhaps the trip can be justified as "necessary," but it's going to be a hard sell—such a hard sell that most employees won't buy it. The trip doesn't appear legitimate— and it certainly doesn't appear inexpensive. Furthermore, does the company really need a helicopter?

That one instance of apparent extravagance will probably nullify all the positive values of the communication program intended to limit expenses. Example is just that powerful.

Well, some executives might say, maybe we can tolerate just a little extravagance for the CEO—after all, she or he has earned it—and, anyway, nobody will ever know. Don't bet on it. I'm not exactly sure how it works, but ABC, NBC, CBS, CNN, and Fox combined can't begin to have the communications impact of the corporate grapevine.

Dr. Carl Menninger of the famed Menninger Foundation, one of the foremost psychiatric hospitals in the United States, has said that the human being is 90% reactive and only 10% intellectual. That's why when you wave, others wave back. When you smile, they smile back. That is how clothing styles begin. Your teenage son wants to dress like other teenage boys, even though he says he wants to be "his own person."

Likewise, people are reactive to their leadership. If you come to work late, they will be late too. If you break the rules, they will too. Everything starts at the top. People tend to be reflections of their leader.

I cannot overemphasize that successful leaders must be successful communicators. Example is the most powerful communicator of all. Setting a positive example requires great commitment and some sacrifice—a commitment that most would-be leaders are not willing to make.

Failing to set the right example is why most would-be leaders fail.

Yes, I know. This is asking a lot. As I've told you before, becoming a great leader isn't easy.

SILVER BULLETS

▲ All forms of communication become relatively ineffective if the leader does not set an appropriate example.

▲ When the leader violates his or her own guidelines, everyone tends to know it, thanks to the good old-fashioned corporate grapevine. All major TV networks can't reach your people as well as the corporate grapevine.

▲ People are reactive. They reflect their leadership.

▲ Example is the most powerful communicator of all. It requires great commitment and sacrifice—which most would-be leaders are not willing to make. This is why most of them fail.

8

A SETTING-AN-EXAMPLE CHECKLIST

There are hundreds—maybe thousands—of little things that the leader must do to set a positive example for others—little things that add up to big things over time. Insignificant? Petty? Possibly so. But they are all meaningful symbols that help the leader establish the company's critical *philosophical framework*. Symbolism plays a big role in leadership. For instance:

FLY WITH THE TROOPS. If you are like me, it seems that you spend half your life on an airplane. It's uncomfortable and it's not fun. If you still think traveling is fun, chances are traveling is not a big part of your work week. Fun or not, it's important that you fly coach.

Even when you've been upgraded with coupons earned with jillions of miles of Flustered Flyer points? Yes, no upgrades if others from your company are on the same plane. Fly with the troops. It's probably not a good idea to move up in any event, because customers, investors, and others with whom you may have contact will assume you are being frivolous with company money. You may not have an opportunity to explain otherwise.

Not long ago I was flying to Minneapolis. Probably noticing my substantial accumulation of frequent-flyer points, the gate agent said, "We have space in first class today. I'll move you up."

"No you won't," I answered.

"Oh, you're the boss," she said.

I was pleased that she knew my situation without asking. Apparently my counterparts in other companies have likewise declined first class upgrades for the same reason.

"I have two associates with me," I continued. "If you can move up all three of us, that would be appreciated." Ultimately she did upgrade all three of us, and my associates felt pampered.

That is just another small but important symbol; everybody in the company plays by the same rules. And that means everybody.

On the other hand, I have been on flights in which subordinates were upgraded to first class while I flew coach. Most expressed embarrassment—but not so much that they refused to accept the upgrade.

JUST PLANE TROUBLE. Speaking of flying, take a hard look at the company plane, if you have one. When I became president of our company in 1983, that was one of the first changes I made— I eliminated the leased company plane.

Frankly, I love to fly on corporate aircraft. We can go when we want—return when we want—and we're treated like humans. What a contrast to the hassle of the commercial airlines that don't have the foggiest notion of what customer service is all about.

Still, the corporate aircraft is too often a symbol of "just plane trouble" in many companies. For instance, our airplane could be cost-justified—allegedly—when there were eight passengers. If those eight people saved eight commercial airline tickets, eight hotel rooms, and 16 meals, it was a break-even deal, with the added bonus of the convenience of traveling on our schedule.

But here's the hitch. You could bet that anyone who needed to make a company trip could, and usually did, scrounge up seven people to go along. I know one officer of a major corporation who took secretaries with him in order to round up the number required to justify using the corporate airplane. Does that make a lot of business sense?

In our case, while those eight people were traveling, they weren't able to work at their headquarters location—and they were bothering eight others at the remote office, so they couldn't work either. Furthermore, often they were key managers whom we should not have been exposing to a single airplane accident. (Incidentally, if you don't have a policy about who can fly with whom, you should. Risk management is a part of your management responsibility. And risk management is more than making sure you have adequate liability and property insurance. No company can afford to lose its most valuable resource—its key people.)

The corporate airplane just may be one of those conveniences that you should do without.

THE BOAR'S HEAD INN: The notes for this particular chapter were made on a note pad from The Boar's Head Inn, Charlottesville, Virginia. In my desk drawer are note pads from perhaps 20 or 30 hotels and conference centers where I have stayed or made a speech over these past several weeks. When I stay in a hotel, I pick up the notepads in the room and toss them in my briefcase.

These are used for my personal use as well as inter-office communications. When I receive a letter that requires action by someone in the organization, I jot a note on the hotel notepad—"Joe, please take a look at this and respond to Mr. Smith." They are also handy for routing newspaper and magazine articles that may be of interest to others.

Why hotel notepads? First, it saves money—not much, but a little. Second, and most important, it sends a signal to our people. Another symbol, if you please. A few cents here and a few cents there add up—which is important in low margin businesses like ours. It also sends a fairly strong message that it isn't necessary to have personalized note pads imprinted "Memo from the desk of . . . "

If you insist on embossed note pads with your initials in platinum, that's OK with me. But expect your people to spend money the same way.

IT'S 8:00 A.M.—WHERE'S THE BOSS? Flextime is popular among American workers today. It's popular among great leaders as well—but it has a different meaning. The real leader flexes in early and flexes out late. (We'll talk more about flextime, for it's important that we accommodate our employees. But it's more important that we serve our customers. No customers, no employees.)

Managers often tell me, "I may come in a little late, but I always work late in the evening."

My response is, "How do your employees know you leave late? They probably assume you leave five minutes after they do."

The bottom line: If you want your employees to work a full day, you must be there when that workday begins. And you must be there when the workday ends.

PARK ANY PLACE YOU WISH: And you *can* park any place you wish—if you get there early enough. That means no assigned parking place. You park in the south 40 like everyone else. Remember, this is a game of symbolism. This is the way corporate cultures are established. Everyone must understand that we all play by the same rules.

THE EXECUTIVE DINING ROOM: I often brag that we have the largest executive dining room in town. It has to be big because we share it with a few hundred others. You got it—no executive dining room. We all play by the same rules here (or have I said that before?).

MAKE YOUR OWN PHONE CALLS: I am offended when I answer my phone and a secretary on the other end of the line says, "Just a moment please. Mr. Jones calling." Mr. Jones is no busier than I am. If I can answer my own phone, he can make his own calls. No business can take the chance of offending a customer.

ANSWER YOUR OWN PHONE: Now for the other side of the equation. Answer your own phone, if you're available. It could even be a call from a disgruntled customer. You need to hear it once in a while—and that disgruntled customer may not be so disgruntled when he or she ends up talking to the top dog. Impressed? You bet.

What, no phone mail? Phone mail has a place in business, but it should be used properly. No activity is more offensive than "phone mail hell." It should be possible for any caller to be connected to a real live human being after one phone-mail greeting. A good rule of thumb—when you find yourself becoming annoyed with the phone mail of people with whom you are trying to do business, your customers are likewise becoming annoyed with your company. We can't afford to annoy a customer.

Keep phone mail menus short. After a dozen menu choices—none of which fit the nature of my call precisely—I forget the previous choices and have to go through the whole schmeel again. Three or four options are all that callers can remember.

Even more maddening—"Please spell the name of the person you are calling using your touch tone phone." Ah, come on! I can call a competitor in less time than it takes me to spell out a name with a phone keypad.

The message here is that most people want to do business with people. The phone should facilitate those people relationships, not impede them.

PRACTICE CONSISTENCY: Everyone gets up on the wrong side of the bed once in a while. We all have bad days now and then. Most of us have our periods of kindness, irritation, anger, and tantrums. If personality traits creep out on occasion, at least they must creep out consistently. Leadership, coaching, and parenting have this in common. Your response to certain conditions should be consistent every time. If your kids do something cute and you laugh the first time and spank them the second time, they get confused. The same is true in leadership. Your reaction should be predictable.

Obviously, kindness and understanding should be a part of your personality makeup whenever possible. But when employees violate important company rules and principles—or violate less important rules and principles the second or third time—it's OK to fly off the handle. It's OK to show that this behavior will not be tolerated. Certain violations will result in immediate termination— such as employee dishonesty. Zero tolerance. No exceptions.

Consistency! React similarly to similar situations every time.

IF YOU'RE GOING TO BE A COWBOY: Not long ago this position would have been considered old fashioned. Now I can say I'm on the cutting edge of a trend, for survey after survey now say that business attire is coming back. In 1999 sales of high-end business suits increased by 30%. Yes! Employees are becoming reluctant to give the impression that they are fugitives from the dot.com world. They are beginning to understand the need to establish the trust and confidence to which professional dress contributes.

Through the years I've been sold on the idea that if you are going to be a cowboy, you should dress like a cowboy. That means if you are going to be a doctor, you should dress like a doctor. (Periodically I see a doctor wearing blue jeans while making his rounds at the hospital, and if I were his patient, I would have somewhat less confidence in him.) If you are going to be a lawyer, dress like a lawyer. And if you are going to be a professional, dress like a professional.

As a professional observer of people for more than 40 years, I'm convinced that professionals tend to be less professional when they are dressed for washing the car. Some believe that the casual dress trend has had the effect of reducing the normal workweek by 20%. Some go so far as to try to avoid certain business transactions on casual Fridays because employees are more error prone. Furthermore, I find it offensive when my business transaction is being handled by a person wearing a *I'm With Stupid* or *One's in the Oven* t-shirt. I just can't believe that my request for service is being given the care I expect. OK, so I lack a sense of humor.

Paul Harvey, the noted newscaster, resides in Arizona in the wintertime. Because of time zones, he must arise in the wee hours to do his early morning newscast. Since he works from his home, he would do that newscast wearing pajamas and a robe. But he noted that something was wrong. He asked an associate if the Harvey edge was gone—if the associate noted a difference. Indeed it was being noticed. Mr. Harvey found that his morning message had a little more oomph when he dressed professionally.

Not long ago, I read that a law firm had conducted a poll and found that 44% of managers noted an increase in tardiness and absenteeism when casual dress was introduced, and 30% detected an increase in flirtatious behavior.

I'm amazed that American business leaders have been snookered by a Dockers Casual Friday promotion—which gradually became Business Casual Every Day—which gradually gave way to Sloppy Every Day. Oh well, McDonald's taught America to bus its own tables, so perhaps we shouldn't be too surprised that we would go along so easily with a Dockers advertising program.

Dress appropriately for your business—and dress the way you want your people to dress.

* * * * *

The "setting an example" checklist could go on for hundreds of pages, but you're getting the gist of it by now. Your company— your department—is a reflection of the leader. What you do, your people do. Every day you send them subtle but powerful messages with the little examples you set.

SILVER BULLETS

▲ A leader sets a positive example for employees in hundreds of ways— all symbols that establish a company's philosophical framework.

▲ Fly coach—we all follow the same rules here.

▲ No personalized note pads are necessary—we all follow the same rules here.

▲ Flex in early and flex out late.

▲ No assigned parking slots—we all follow the same rules here.

▲ Make and take your own phone calls.

▲ Always be consistent.

▲ Dress the way you want your employees to dress.

▲ Oh yes! We all follow the same rules here.

Get Ready, Get Set, Communicate

9

CREATING A NEW CORPORATE CULTURE

Most would agree that we started out with a sleepy old company. Some would say stagnant. Our mission was to build a new company—a new corporate culture—through an aggressive program of open communication. This is after 60 years of being a secretive, non-communicative organization. The plan was to establish a policy of fully informing employees about everything—that means *every*thing—with only two exceptions. The exceptions were quarterly earnings before they were announced to the investor community at large and the acquisition of another company or a piece of property being negotiated under a confidentiality agreement. Employees were (and still are) told that everything else is on the table.

Today a change has taken place. The company is progressive, innovative, efficient and successful. Employee morale is high. Turnover is low. Hiring new people is not a problem, even in a near-no-unemployment economy.

What's the secret? I would like to be able to give you the family recipe, including the blend of secret herbs and spices, which will turn it around fast. But I can't. We used a combination of communication devices and techniques. Some worked and others probably didn't. But all the messages were essentially the same. Everyone was singing from the same hymnbook.

It starts out with a vision. No, not one of those vision statements that's published in the back of a company's annual report. Most of them are so general that they're meaningless.

I'm talking about a picture of the company. What will it look like in five years? And why? And the employees must understand what's in it for them. The picture must be so vivid that you can see it in your mind's eye. Can you paint this picture so clearly that your people can see it as clearly as you do? It may take a while.

If the company is in trouble—i.e., it's having difficulties meeting the payroll and everybody knows it—you may need to hit the ground running. But, normally it's a good idea to take the time to ask for help from the real experts—the employees who are closer to your customers and the day-to-day activities than you are. Start off with a general meeting, then meet one on one. And do it regularly. Ask each one, "If you were promoted to my job, what would you do first—and second—etc.? Make notes. When the vision statement is complete, chances are it will encompass many—maybe even most—of the suggestions your people have made.

Don't be too alarmed if your requests for suggestions are not met with overwhelming enthusiasm. After all, most people have never before been asked for their ideas. And many will be suspicious of your motives.

My company had employees scattered in several states. Through the years we had held meetings with independent insurance agents (independent contractors who sell our products) throughout those states without inviting our own employees from an office six blocks down the street. Many times we had not even informed our employees that such meetings were being held.

When I became president of the company, I invited those outlying employees to a breakfast or luncheon where we could answer their questions and solicit their suggestions. What could we do to respond to their needs? What were their suggestions for improving our operations? What could we do to make their lives easier?

Almost without exception, the group sat quietly, arms folded. Every eye in the place seemed to say, "I don't like you. I don't trust you. I know you're not having this meeting for the fun of it—now cut out the BS and give me the bad news. I know there is going to be bad news. You're closing our office. You're pulling out of this state. Hurry up and tell us."

This is normal resistance. You see, most of those folks had never before been asked to meetings such as this without hearing bad news, like office closings or layoffs. And if you, the manager, have been around the company for a while, suspicion is even greater. "Why is the boss acting this way? Is the company in financial difficulty?" You can bet the assumptions will be negative—it's inherent in the human makeup.

But there was no bad news. When the meetings ended, I generally felt I had walked out of the freezer at the local butcher shop.

A few months later we tried it again; two-way communication improved a bit. We did it again a few months later—and communication improved again. We were still seeing communication barriers breaking down three years later.

When jobs are at stake and the very survival of the company is being threatened, the change can be made to occur somewhat more rapidly. But that's an alternative most of us would prefer to avoid. It's much easier to change a relatively healthy company slowly than to try to pull an unhealthy company out of the fire rapidly.

There's probably no way to short-cut the process. Just communicate, communicate, communicate.

The new spirit, enthusiasm, work ethic, innovativeness, efficiency, progressiveness, and success of your company will be worth the effort—and the wait.

SILVER BULLETS

▲ The mission is to build a new corporate culture through an aggressive program of open communication.

▲ Employees are told *everything*.

▲ Use a number of communication devices and techniques. Some will work, others won't.

▲ All messages are essentially the same. Everyone sings out of the same hymnbook.

▲ Paint a picture of the company—how will it look in five years? And why? What's in it for your employees?

▲ Resistance is normal. Keep on communicating.

▲ The new company is worth the effort and the wait.

10
HAVE I TOLD YOU THE ONE ABOUT . . . ?

We tell 'em . . . and tell 'em . . . and tell 'em. And it works.

When any unusual problem or circumstance comes along, I'm confident that at least 98% of the time any one of our management people would make the decision that I would.

Management gurus talk about and encourage empowerment and delegation. But unless there is a clear vision—unless the philosophical framework of the company is well understood—the actions of the many people throughout the company may be inconsistent. Your company may be establishing one reputation with one client and an entirely different reputation with another client.

Once the company vision and philosophical framework are clearly understood, use every conceivable communication technique known to mankind to get the message out.

In our company, senior management meets every Monday morning—at 7:00 a.m. There is a short agenda—and every attendee is asked to give an update of what is going on in his or her department. It's a time to hash-out problems that overlap departments. The meeting adjourns at 8:00 a.m.

The Monday morning time slot was chosen for several reasons: (1) senior management travel schedules are less likely to conflict; (2) senior management hits the ground running every week—this is another symbol; and (3) optimists get up early and pessimists get up late (I believe it was basketball coach Rick Pitino who said that).

Monthly in the home office and four times a year in outlying offices, we hold President's Open Forums. Attendance is not mandatory, but most employees in our outlying offices attend. Because of the larger employee population in the home office, everyone does not attend, but we usually have standing room only. The employee grapevine generally carries the message to several others, so we reach a good number of employees each month.

Periodically there is a gripe—usually a legitimate one. On one occasion, I was told of a tree in one of the parking lots that produced some kind of a berry that stained cars parked there. That very day, the buildings and grounds manager and I visited that parking lot and found the tree. The next day it was gone. (My apologies to the tree-huggers.)

For the most part, however, there are no gripes. Instead there is genuine interest in the company, its direction, how industry problems are being dealt with, how we intend to respond to the actions of our competitors, and similar weighty matters. Employees at all levels want to be a part of—and want to contribute to—a successful organization.

All managers are asked to get out of their offices. Talk to their people. Listen to their people.

Every week I tried to spend at least two hours covering one wing of the building. One week I would wander through Fourth Floor

East, next week Fourth Floor West, next week Third Floor East, etc. I tried to talk to every employee who was at his or her workstation and was not on the phone. Perhaps this is somewhat of an exaggeration, but I believe each week I was able to pay for my annual salary by acting on things I learned during those weekly rounds.

The answer was "Fine," when I asked "How are you doing?" But when I asked, "What can we do to make your job easier?" I often got a very helpful answer. One long-time underwriting assistant told me that reinsurance on cars valued at more than $50,000 was a pain in the you-know-what. This was the only non-automated function she had to deal with, and it certainly wasn't her favorite activity.

"Reinsurance?" I asked. "Why are you buying reinsurance on $50,000 cars?"

"That's what they told me to do when I came here," she answered.

She "came here" many years ago, when the company was quite small—and when $50,000 was a significant amount of money. In the meantime, the company had grown and inflation had taken its toll. At this point the company was assuming $2 million of insurance risk, not $50,000.

I talked to the underwriting director (who likewise didn't know we were doing this) and we solved the problem immediately. Savings amounted to hundreds of thousands of dollars each year.

Nearly every week I found something that could be improved—that would improve customer service—that would bring about significant savings.

Get out of your office! See your people! Face-to-face communication. That's the most effective form of communication. I often threatened to fill our managers' offices with concrete—"and when we do, I hope you're not still in it," I told the occupants.

Supplement all these forms of direct communication with the more formal forms of communication—all the things that PR departments think they have to do to earn their keep.

For example, use newsletters. Now we put one out on the company intranet and update it daily. Another feature of the intranet is *forum.bob* through which employees company-wide can ask questions, anonymously if they wish. All questions are answered—no screening.

And there are company-produced audiotapes and videotapes, although I'm not a real believer in videotapes. Most Americans are now accustomed to professionalism in that medium, and most managers come through on video as rank amateurs.

The messages contained in all these forms of communication must always be consistent—always driving home the culture of the company, the objectives of the company, and every bit of information possible to make the employees feel like owners.

SILVER BULLETS

▲ Empowerment and delegation are ineffective if there is no clear vision of company's direction and philosophy.

▲ Face-to-face communication is best—including management meetings and open forums with employees.

▲ Supplement face-to-face communications with the more formal forms of communication—like newsletters, company intranet, audiotapes and videotapes.

▲ All messages must be consistent—driving home the culture and objectives of the company.

11

SIT, SIT, SIT, SIT, SIT, SIT, SIT, SIT, SIT, SIT, SIT

Several years ago, there was an ad in *The Wall Street Journal* that consisted of a series of panels of a dog standing, each with the caption "sit." In the final panel the dog was finally sitting, with the caption "Good dog."

I misplaced the ad long ago, and I don't remember its sponsor. I apologize for not being able to give proper credit. On dozens of occasions, I carried the ad to management staff meetings when I believed that certain aspects of our corporate policy or objectives needed repeating.

Repetition is necessary to get any message across. Repetition is necessary to get any message across. Repetition is necessary to get any message across. Repetition is necessary to . . . You know that, don't you?

Is there a man, woman, or child in America who has not heard of McDonald's? Most of us have eaten Big Macs. We know what to expect when we go into a McDonald's. We know something about price levels. We know something about the cleanliness we can expect. Kids know they will get toys with their Happy Meals. Yet McDonald's still runs commercials. Why? They know that repetition is necessary to keep the McDonald's name in the minds of their customers.

Most of us stop communicating a needed message because we are tired of it, not because it no longer has value. Advertising experts tell us that some of the world's best commercials stop running at about the time they are having the greatest impact on prospective buyers—because the sponsor is tired of it, not because the buyer is tired of it.

As a matter of fact, the sudden absence of the message is usually interpreted as a change of company policy or focus—"they must not be interested in that anymore." Time and again, we have found a problem in our company that must be addressed. A solution is developed and work begins. The communication continues for three months—or six months. We're well on our way to fixing the problem. Then the communication stops. Six months later we look back over our shoulder and find that we solved part of the problem but not all of it. When we ask why the job wasn't completed, the answer is, "I didn't think the company was interested in that anymore."

Keep in mind that the mission hadn't changed. It was just that the message hadn't been repeated lately.

One way to keep the message fresh is for the leader to use new stories. Be an active reader. Read about other industries and about other leaders. You'll see parallels to your own business. You can use those stories to give a new look and a new feel to the same underlying messages that are so important to your people.

Never stop communicating. Keep driving home those company values, objectives, and philosophies. Repetition is necessary to make the company culture second nature to every member of the company team.

Remember, McDonald's still runs commercials.

Sit, sit, sit, sit, sit, sit, sit, sit, sit sit, sit.

SILVER BULLETS

▲ Repetition is necessary to get any message across.

▲ Most managers stop communicating because they are tired of the message, not because the message doesn't have value.

▲ The absence of a message for a period of time is usually interpreted as a change of company policy—"they must not be interested in that anymore."

▲ Keep the same underlying message fresh by using new stories.

▲ Repetition makes the corporate culture second nature to every member of the company team.

12

THE MANAGEMENT RICHTER SCALE

The Richter Scale records the magnitude of earthquakes. Each point on the scale represents a tenfold increase in energy over the previous point. In communication there is an equivalent of the Richter Scale. For every level of management through which communication must take place, the difficulty of achieving good communication is greatly increased. That's why I call it *The Management Richter Scale*.

Most companies I visit have too many layers of management. At one time, my company had too many layers. We had departments in which the manager had as few as two or three direct reports—in a few situations one direct report. You can be certain that in a one-to-one reporting relationship, and in most cases in a two- or three-to-one reporting relationship, somebody is unnecessary. (Tip: Start looking at those individuals with a title of Assistant

Manager.) Those additional management layers are expensive—and they hamper communication. Every management layer adds one more opportunity for information to be screened—or spun.

We adopted a policy of never having more than five layers from top to bottom. Never. Most departments have even fewer levels. It's simple to do the math. Five layers of management can properly manage a huge corporation with several thousand employees. For many years I had 12 vice presidents reporting to me. Too many? If they are competent people who can be trusted, it's not too many. How can you determine the number of layers required? Start by figuring 12 direct reports per manager. Some managers can easily oversee 20 or more, especially if there are "lead workers" who can help train new employees, distribute work, etc. For some it may be five or six, depending on the complexity of the operation and travel distances that may be required. But 12 is a good place to start. Now adjust the 12 direct reports upward or downward depending on the circumstances. This will give you an idea of the number of managers required.

Not long ago Toyota cut more than 20 layers of management down to eleven. General Motors used to have 28 layers. The last I knew, it was down to 19. It seems to me they have a way to go.

A span of control that is too wide is more desirable than an unnecessary layer of management. Most employees will agree. They want to be heard by senior management, and they don't like the frustration of trying to communicate through too many layers. If a suggestion actually makes it through the process, they know that some manager along the line will take credit for it. Most likely, however, some manager in the communication chain will have a "don't rock the boat" mentality, and the great idea will never see the light of day. It's maddening to work in companies like that.

How do we get into this too-many-layers mess? Often it's a way managers recognize their good subordinates by giving them titles (and possibly a way to reduce their own work loads). Then there comes a day when excessive payroll consumes the company. That leads to a process called "downsizing" or "rightsizing" in which many people in middle management get the ax. Often they are good people who do not deserve to be treated that way.

Keeping the layers of management at the minimum possible level helps to avoid unnecessary overhead costs, keep the company focused, avoid bureaucratic deadlock, and make the company more responsive, sure-footed, and successful.

. . . and it avoids a major impediment to good communication.

SILVER BULLETS

▲ For every level of management, the difficulty of communication greatly increases.

▲ A one-to-one or two- or three-to-one reporting relationship is seldom necessary.

▲ It's more desirable to have a span of control that is too wide than an unnecessary layer of management.

13
THE INFORMED MANAGER

"You're a hands-on manager," I'm often told.

"Perhaps I am," I answer, "but I prefer to be called an informed manager. In my view, there isn't any difference between a hands-on manager and an informed manager."

Let's get back to basics. The foundation of leadership (and the overall field of management as well) is communication. If you're going to build a team, that team has to know what's going on and must be willing to let others know what's going on. That means the sales department must know what's going on in the IT department (a fancy name for the computer people); and the IT department must know what's going on in the claims department; and the claims department must know what's going on in the underwriting department; and so on. And each of those departments must understand its role in bringing about appropriate solutions.

It's not possible for a company to act like a company if each department is independent of the other departments. That's like the head coach telling his football team, "OK, guys. Get out there and run your favorite play. I've got a tee-time in 30 minutes. Let me know how the game turns out."

I'm willing to bet that that team won't win many games. Nor will the corporation win many games if department heads don't communicate with one another. And it certainly won't win many games if the leader is ill-informed.

As the leader, you're the head coach. You want all departments to be informed about what's going on in the rest of the company and the industry overall. Everyone has to understand the big picture. Everyone has to understand the objectives of the company; its priorities; its problems; how those problems must be dealt with; the actions of competitors and how the company intends to respond. Everything must fit together. Every department must play a role. And the roles played by the various departments must be compatible with one another.

How can a department play an appropriate role if it doesn't understand all the facts? If it doesn't understand the company and the industry and all the intricate pieces of the puzzle?

Now, back to the leader. How can a leader lead when he or she doesn't have an understanding of that big picture, those problems, and the roles of the various departments in solving those problems?

Being an informed manager has nothing to do with unwillingness to delegate or insistence on dictating decisions. It has to do with people in the appropriate departments making decisions based on a comprehensive understanding of the complete picture.

In all my years in management, there have been only a handful of instances in which I have dictated decisions (although I have slowed down other's decisions that I thought were being made without sufficient information). When people have full information—and when they operate within the same philosophical framework—the decision generally emerges to the satisfaction of everyone.

Of the thousands of leaders I've observed during my years as a professional people watcher, the informed leaders are the most effective leaders. They are more likely to run the successful companies that survive and prosper through the years.

SILVER BULLETS

▲ There isn't any difference between a hands-on manager and an informed manager.

▲ All departments must understand the big picture, the company objectives, its priorities, its problems, the competitors, how the company intends to respond, and the role each department must play.

▲ A department cannot play an appropriate role if it doesn't understand all the facts.

▲ Being an informed leader has nothing to do with an unwillingness to delegate or an insistence on dictating decisions.

▲ When people have full information—and operate within the same philosophical framework—the right decisions generally emerge.

14
WHISSSSHHH!

That's the air being released from the balloons of irate callers—whether employees, customers, or other upset people with whom leaders have to deal with from time to time. In a company with open communication—where the CEO answers his or her own phone—where leaders walk the buildings to talk to people—where leaders meet with salespeople and customers as often as possible—leaders need to know how to deal with irate people.

There's a way to release the pressure from their emotional balloons and get them back to a rational state of mind. The method works—guaranteed. When the conversations conclude, the complainant still may not agree with your position, but the discussions will have been conducted in a cool, calm, and rational manner.

Upset people who approach you just *know* that you are going to be unreasonable. They *know* you are going to argue. They *know* you are going to be force-ful with your response. So they unload on you with both barrels. Pow!

What do you do? You surprise them. You listen. And listen. And listen. Nod your head periodically. It's not a signal that you are agreeing; it's a signal that you are listening.

Listen until the air is out of their balloon. This may take some time, but it's always worthwhile to restore rationality to the debate.

Finally, they stop. They have expressed their arguments. They're out of gas. Their balloon is completely limp. Wait for a few seconds and ask a question, any question, that might shed further light on the situation—such as, "When did this occur?" The significance of the question is not important. They expected you to argue, but you do not. You asked a question instead. This says to the irate individual, "Hey, this guy is more reasonable than I thought he would be."

Then you ask a second question. And the third. And the fourth. Make sure all the facts have been expressed by the complaining party. Make sure the other person has not been cut off without hav-ing had an opportunity to get the matter off his or her chest. Even though you can answer the concern much earlier in the conversa-tion, you must hear out the argument. Completely.

Then hesitate for a few seconds and say, "I understand how you feel." You did not say, "I agree with you," because you may not agree. But you can understand how they feel.

Then you can start responding to the concern, laying out all the facts in a logical sequence, always in a calm tone of voice.

Then apologize for the inconvenience or the misunderstanding. If it involves something that the company mishandled, give them assurance that you will look into the matter and do what is neces-sary to avoid it happening in the future. If the company didn't do anything wrong, apologize for the misunderstanding.

"I'm not going to apologize," many say, "because I didn't do anything wrong."

Apologize anyway. It simply doesn't cost anything to apologize. And you're not being dishonest—you're saying "If you misunderstood something we've done, I'm truly sorry you misunderstood."

Now—thank the complainant for calling the matter to your attention. That's a sincere act too. I always want to know what our employees and customers are thinking, even when it's something not very pleasant. If something is bugging them, I want to know. Don't you?

Listen, listen, listen. Ask a question, ask a question, ask a question. "I understand how you feel." Try it—it works.

SILVER BULLETS

▲ When approached by an irate person, listen…listen…listen. Nod your head periodically as a signal that you're listening.

▲ When that person has fully stated his or her case, ask a question. Then a second, third, and fourth question.

▲ Next, say that you know how the person feels. Even though you don't agree with the position being expressed, you can still understand how he or she feels.

▲ Then respond to the complaint point by point, in a calm, rational manner.

▲ Finally, apologize for the inconvenience or misunderstanding. It never costs anything to apologize.

15
THANK YOU

My flight was late and I arrived at my hotel at about 10:00 p.m. I was hungry (the bag of peanuts on the plane didn't satisfy my need for nourishment) and tired (I get up at 5:00 a.m., so by 10 p.m. I'm tired)

The Marriott desk clerk gave me the room key; I put my bag on my shoulder (at that time the only ones smart enough to have wheels on their luggage were airline people) and took the elevator to my room. I fiddled with the magnetic key but couldn't get the door open.

I put my bag on my shoulder and returned to the desk. The agent checked the key and said, "I'm sorry, sir. I gave you the wrong key."

With the new key in hand, I put my bag on my shoulder and took the elevator to my room. Once again, I could not get the door open.

I put my bag on my shoulder and returned to the desk. The agent sort of rolled his eyes, as if to say this guy is too dumb to use these new-fangled keys, and said, "Sir, I will show you."

He took the key and I followed, with my bag on my shoulder, as we took the elevator to my room. He fiddled with the key for a while and said, "The lock must be broken. We will find you a new room." This time he put my bag on his shoulder as we returned to the desk for a key to another room.

Yes, I was a little upset with the Marriott desk clerk—until I got back from a late dinner and found a fruit bowl in my room with a little note signed by the desk clerk, "Mr. Bailey, we apologize for the inconvenience during your check-in this evening. We hope your stay is most pleasant."

The fruit was good—but the handwritten note was especially appreciated, and I have become an unofficial, unpaid ambassador of Marriott.

When I got back to my office, I ordered blank note cards with the company logo on the front, like those used by Marriott. Every week, I send out handwritten notes to several people whose good deeds should be acknowledged. A note to the top sales person who had an especially good month—"Jill, that's the way to go. Thank you. We appreciate you." Or to a claims person who settled a particularly difficult case favorably—"Sam, you did a fantastic job on the Smith claim. Thank you. We appreciate you."

Or to an agent whose son was involved in an automobile accident. Or . . . the list is endless.

I've sent out hundreds of copies of a little booklet called *One Man's Miracle,* published by the Peale Foundation for Christian Living, to people who have been diagnosed with cancer.

These little notes are not expensive. They don't require much time. And they are strong signals that you care about people.

There was a time when professionally prepared typewritten letters would have had more impact. But in these days of word processing, when "standard" letters can be turned out by the hundred and look personalized, nothing has more impact than brief handwritten notes.

In this "dog-eat-dog" business world, business people too often think they don't have time for such foolishness. "I'm much too busy for that," some say. A leader, however, recognizes the value of a "thank you."

On one flight, I was served a drink by the flight attendant and I said "thank you." Later she offered a refill and I said "thank you." Before landing she picked up the empty cup and I said "thank you."

"You just have to be the most courteous passenger we've ever had," the flight attendant said. I doubt if that's true, but it's shocking to me that the flight attendant was impressed with someone who said "thank you" a total of three times. Maybe more of us should practice saying "thank you" a little more.

And, "You're welcome." Too many respond to a thank you with "sure", "uh huh," or nothing at all.

Busy people—and great leaders—always have time to say thank you—and express concern about an illness. Both orally and in writing.

SILVER BULLETS

▲ Handwritten notes are not expensive—they don't require much time—and they are strong signals that you care about people.

▲ In these days of word processing, when "standard" letters can be turned out by the hundred and look personalized, nothing has more impact than a brief handwritten note.

▲ Busy people—and great leaders—always have time to say thank you or to express concern about an illness. Orally and in writing.

16
JUST SAY NO

Most of us have never learned to say *no* with class. We tell our people that we want suggestions to improve operations, ideas to speed service, or ways to reduce expenses. When they respond, we may just say *no* and devastate the person making the suggestion. "That's the only suggestion they'll ever get from me," he or she will decide.

There is a more kind, more gentle way of saying "no." We can learn something from the Japanese, who have 19 different ways of saying "no." In their language, the verb appears at the end of the sentence, because the speaker wants so much to avoid conflict. The listener doesn't know where the speaker is going until the end of the sentence. So, the speaker can change verbs midstream in response to the listener's expression and body language.

For instance, a banker might say, "As to your loan request, it is my observation that as to your eligibility for a loan you would . . ." The banker would be watching the applicant's expression. If the loan applicant looks hostile, he would end the sentence "qualify." Or if the applicant appeared to know that there was a better chance of winning $100 million in the state lottery than to get this loan, the banker would say "not qualify."

Other than the Japanese, my predecessor, Paul Gingher, could say *no* better than anybody in the universe. If I went to him with a rather stupid suggestion (which I was quite capable of doing), he would ask a few questions—enough to make me understand that I really hadn't thought it through very well. Then he would say, "You know, I have another appointment in five minutes," as he looked at his watch. "Let's think about it."

Then, as he stood up to make his appointment (which I don't think he really had), he would say, "Give some thought to these points," as he listed four or five dimensions that I hadn't considered. "Let's get together at 1:30 on Thursday and talk about it again," he would conclude.

When we talked about it next Thursday, normally I had done a much better job of evaluating the matter and normally had come around to his position. Yes, experience does matter.

He always got "buy-ins" from his people, without crushing them with a harsh veto.

"Let's think about it"—a great way to get your people to rethink an emerging decision that you're uncomfortable with. "Think about these points and we'll meet on this topic next week."

SILVER BULLETS

▲ Saying no to ideas or suggestions may strangle employees' willingness to make suggestions in the future.

▲ The challenge is to get "buy-ins" from your people without crushing them with harsh vetoes.

▲ "Let's think about it"—a great way to get your people to rethink an emerging decision that you're uncomfortable with.

17

WHEN YOU SAY IT—
HOW YOU SAY IT

When you say it—how you say it. It's all a part of communication.

THE RITZ-CARLTON TRAINING PRO-GRAM: There's something special about Ritz-Carlton. While ordering lunch at poolside at the Ritz-Carlton in Naples, Florida, I said to the waitress, "There's something special about the training program of personnel here. Can you tell me about your training?"

"Well, primarily it's on-the-job training," she said. "The formal training really pertains to what we can't say rather than what we can say."

"What you can't say?" I asked.

"Yes," she continued. "We can't say *hi*—it's *good morning madam* or *sir*. We can't say *yeow*—it's *yes madam* or *yes sir*. When a customer gives an order, it's *it is my pleasure sir*."

The last time I was in Bermuda, I found rude or non-responding taxi drivers and hotel clerks. Our dinner reservation was cancelled (and no effort was made to rectify it) because *the girl on the last shift made a mistake*. And—guess what—tourism is declining.

There's a lesson here for all of us.

UNHAPPY HOLIDAYS: I've found that the holiday season— around Christmas and New Year's Day—is not a great time to announce reorganizations, restructuring, or other significant changes in the operations. Generally it can be done at some other time of the year just as easily. Too many announcements of new developments are deliberately held back for two or three months in order to hit a January 1 date, as if a project's success is dependent upon Baby New Year.

This is hard to understand. For some reason, there are more deaths, more suicides, and more general unhappiness around the holiday season than at other times of the year. Perhaps during the holidays many folks are thinking about family, friends, and others who are worse off than they are. Perhaps too many over-extend financially, buying things they simply cannot afford.

Through careful planning, major announcements usually can be scheduled for a time when your people can best accept them without adversely affecting the company. A happy work force pays off in many ways.

IMAGINING THE WORST: Whenever there is an information void, people imagine the worst. It's human nature.

Let's say a job is being phased out. You call in the affected person and tell him or her that the job is being discontinued, "but don't worry. We will be offering you a job elsewhere in the company. We don't yet know what you'll be doing, but we'll find something for you over the next four or five weeks."

Despite that assurance, the person will fume, fret, lose sleep and will imagine the worst possible set of circumstances.

On the other hand, if you tell the person whose job is being discontinued, "Bill, the work you are performing is being eliminated through automation. But we like you and have respect for your abilities, so we want to keep you as a part of our organization. We don't have an appropriate job that fully utilizes your talents right now, but we do have a job in mail distribution that we would like for you to work until an appropriate job opens up."

Undoubtedly Bill won't like the prospect of working in mail distribution, but my experience is that Bill will have less worry and stress knowing where he will be assigned than he would if left dangling for the next few weeks.

The unknown has a way of causing people to imagine the worst.

IT'S TEMPORARY: Many of our announcements contain statements like this: "Temporarily this activity will be handled in this manner." Or, "Bill Jones has been temporarily given this responsibility."

"Why do you make so many temporary assignments?" one of our officers once asked.

"Webster says temporary means 'a limited time'," I answered. "Everything is temporary. Life itself is temporary. To me temporary means some period of time between one second and 100 years."

In all the years that I have made "temporary" assignments, I can recall only the one incident in which the temporary nature of the assignment was questioned.

I like temporary assignments simply because it's easier for me to correct my mistakes.

If a new procedure does not work out as well as we thought, we can change it and indicate that this replaces the temporary procedure put into place several months ago. If a person does not work out on the new job, the announcement states that the new person replaces the individual who has been temporarily serving in that role the past six months.

When we make temporary assignments, we don't necessarily immediately start looking for the "permanent" replacements. If the temporary person works out well, that person will be asked to assume the assignment "permanently." If the person does not work out, the "temporary" label helps us correct the mistake while still protecting the person's self esteem.

Of the dozens—and perhaps hundreds—of temporary assignments we have made, the persons asked to accept the temporary assignment never questioned it. Our explanation went something like this: "Betty, here's what we would like you to do temporarily. See what you can do with it and see how you like it. If you're happy with it, we can make a permanent assignment later. If you find that this is not what you want to do with your life, we'll find someone else to do it and you can go back to your present job. But, in the meantime, we believe you're the one who can help us jump-start this project or get this department on track."

This is an insurance policy for the manager—and it's an insurance policy for the employee, who normally has more uncertainty about accepting the new assignment than you have about giving it.

Managers who never make people mistakes need not worry about making temporary assignments; they're always going to select the perfect candidate. However, managers who claim never to have made people mistakes are either not evaluating their employees well or are having a bit of a struggle with honesty. Everybody makes people mistakes.

Temporary assignments provide opportunities for us to get it right the second time.

RUMOR HAS IT: "There should be no rumors in our company," I often told employees in our Open Forums. "We're going to tell you everything—everything—except two things: earnings before they are announced to the investor community and acquisitions being considered under confidentiality agreements.

"When you have questions, call or send an e-mail. If we know the answer we'll tell you," I repeated frequently.

Yet still there were rumors. Every time someone's office door is closed, it seems there are more rumors. No doubt about it, people love rumors and office gossip.

Rumors, too, are a form of communication—a form that must be dealt with. What's the best way to handle it? Announce every new development as soon as it is firmed up. When you know, they should know.

A new manager has been selected for a branch office. You offer the job to the candidate (now two people know—you and the candidate); the candidate talked to his or her spouse (now three people know—you, the candidate, and the candidate's spouse). Since it involves a move to another city, their two kids know (now five people know). The two kids each have three best friends (now 11 people know). And the six friends have 18 best friends, one whose parent works at your company. (That makes . . .) Well, you get the idea. Secrets can't be secrets very long.

Make the announcement to the company at large just as soon as the decision is firm. There is seldom a need for secrecy in any company.

LEAK IT: Having said that there is seldom a need for secrecy and that there is little reason for rumors, the office grapevine can be a part of the company's communications policy. Politicians use this system expertly.

Politicians and boat owners have something in common—the politician wants a bigger, more powerful job; the boat owner wants a bigger, more powerful boat. But politicians often "test the water" before they announce to the world that they are seeking the new job. The test balloon is released—"an informed source" says that politician Brown intends to run for the U.S. Senate. Then they wait to see how other politicians, the media, and the public react.

When politician Brown is asked to confirm the rumor, he says, "Many people have been asking me to run for the U.S. Senate. I'm considering it but have not yet made a decision."

If the public reaction is not favorable, he says that he is perfectly happy in his present job and never intended to run for the Senate anyway.

A few months after our company became publicly owned, I suggested that we give each employee five shares of stock for Christmas in lieu of a package of gifts that had been a tradition for many years. Most of our senior officers and HR people didn't think it would work.

"Most of our people—especially the clerical people—don't want stock," I was told. "Most have never owned any stock in their lives, and they'll never be happy with our stock. In fact, they'll be pretty unhappy if they have to give up the regular Christmas package."

I was clearly on the losing end of this issue. "OK," I said, "let's leak it."

Just a few people—in addition to the officers and Human Resources group—were told that we were considering company stock as a Christmas gift. We waited for a few days and the feedback began—from various home office departments, from outlying branch offices. We could not have purchased television ads that would have been more effective. Comments were 100% positive, incidentally.

We have been giving shares of stock as Christmas gifts every year since. About 10% sell their stock, preferring cash to stock. Still, I'm happy that 90% of our people are legitimate owners of a piece of our company.

Here's a decision that most of our people didn't feel comfortable with. By leaking it, we added a dimension of comfort.

The leader uses every conceivable communication vehicle to get messages out. Leadership *is* communication.

SILVER BULLETS

▲ The holiday season is not the best time to announce major reorganizations, restructuring, and the like.

▲ Significant announcements should be made at a time when employees can more readily accept them.

▲ When there is an information void, people imagine the worst. Keep employees "in the know."

▲ Temporary assignments make it easier for leaders to correct mistakes; they provide comfort to employees who usually have more uncertainty about accepting new assignments than you have about giving them.

▲ People love rumors and office gossip. Keep them to a minimum by making announcements as soon as decisions are made.

▲ Even though there is seldom a need for secrecy in an organization, the office grapevine can be an effective part of a company communication policy.

▲ The leader uses every conceivable communication vehicle to get messages out. Leadership is communication.

SECTION V

What About Me?

18

IF YOU HATE TO GO TO WORK TOMORROW . . .

. . . don't go. For years I have given this message to employees. Successful people can be successful only when they love what they're doing.

What does this have to do with building a corporate culture, with communicating company objectives, with building a philosophical framework? Simply, it's not possible to build a successful operation if employees aren't reasonably happy with their jobs. Those who hate what they're doing—hate their industry—hate the company—hate the boss—hate everything about the place—should look elsewhere for work. Their staying does not help themselves or the company. You can be assured that unhappy people—and people you treat poorly—will not treat your customers the way you would want them to be treated. Fortunately, they are a small percentage of the overall employee population.

Most employees don't hate to go to work. As a matter of fact, most employees enjoy going to work—at least until bad managers change their attitudes.

Even employees who enjoy going to work have special interests. They are all asking, "What about me? What about me and my family and the people in my life whom I'm most concerned about." That's as it should be. It's not a symptom of greed or of lack of commitment. God intended for each of us to take care of ourselves.

If employees believe we do not care about them, it will be difficult for them to take care of the company and to help carry out the company's mission.

So CARE. Care about the people for whom you are responsible. Legitimately care. Ask about a wife who is in the hospital. Ask about the kids in college. Ask about the swim meet in which one of the children participated this past weekend. For those people reporting direct to you, you should know the names of the spouses, the names of the children, their hobbies, any serious health concerns, and even the names of their pets. We have an employee whose dog, Molly, is as much a member of the family as a child. When Molly gets sick, everybody in the family gets sick.

The employees in your company have virtually every problem known to mankind. Some are so severe that you wonder how they are able to cope with them. Other problems are less severe, and they still struggle. Your role is not to intrude but to be a willing, caring ear when the need arises.

One employee came to me following what she thought was an unfair job evaluation by her immediate supervisor. I listened for a few minutes and found that her mother was opposing her upcoming marriage. I asked, "Do you believe this has affected your work?" She agreed that it had. In another case, an employee came to me when her immediate manager said she had a bad attitude after an excellent track record for several years. I found that she had two high-school-age children. Her husband had been off work for more than a year. He found a job, worked two weeks as a roofer, had fallen off a roof, and now was injured and out of work again. During his period of unemployment they had to borrow money to pay alimony to his ex-wife.

"You have a lot of problems," I sympathized.

"Oh yes. I don't know how I can live with all of them," she answered.

"When you feel you need to talk to someone, may I suggest you say to Teresa (her immediate supervisor), 'Teresa, I know you're busy. But I have some problems I would like to talk about. If you don't have time, could you recommend someone I can talk to?'"

Incidentally, this employee (the "bad attitude" now behind her) remained an excellent employee and went on to earn several promotions.

There are computer programs in which you can make notes of personal items about your people as the information comes out in casual conversation—or you can use old faithful 4″ × 6″ cards. The cards work just as well and, for me, are a lot easier to use.

A productive work place must be a caring environment, a fun environment, never an intimidating environment. Does this mean the work place is fun and games and not hard work? A lot more hard work and discipline come out of a pleasant work environment than a hostile work environment. Guaranteed.

SILVER BULLETS

▲ If you hate to go to work tomorrow, don't go. Successful people can be successful only when they love what they're doing.

▲ Most employees enjoy going to work—but they have special interests: "What about me—and my family?"

▲ Leaders care about their people.

▲ A productive work place is a caring environment, a fun environment.

19

THE PERFECT JOB

What do employees want? Most want the *perfect* job. That applies, incidentally, to people at all age levels, whether they're starting out with a new career after college or whether they've been on the job for 20 or 25 years.

This is not a scientific study as such, but I don't think it is an exaggeration to say that over the past 35 or 40 years I've talked to 300 employees who have come to me because they don't like their jobs, they don't like their bosses—they don't like something about their employment situations.

My standard question is, "If we could unbottle a genie who instantly could give you the perfect job, what would it be?" In most cases that question is met with silence or "I don't know."

My questioning continues, "If you won twenty million dollars in the state lottery and you don't need to work, what would you do?" I ask.

The most frequent answer is, "I'd travel."

"OK, you'll travel for three months—or perhaps six months—and you'll get tired of it. I know, because I got tired of it. Then what would you do?" I continue.

In nearly every case the answer is, "I don't know."

"What did you dream about when you were a little girl (or little boy)?" I ask.

Most can answer that question. But it seems that most stopped dreaming at a very young age.

"If you can figure out what you would do if you didn't need to work—something that you love so much that it doesn't seem like work, you'll be successful," my advice continues. That's probably the reason for the success of Sam Walton, the founder of Wal-Mart, and Ray Kroc of McDonald's fame. They truly loved what they were doing so much that they didn't consider it work.

Most of our people, of course, are not budding Waltons or Krocs. As leaders, we must find other means to make the various jobs around our companies as perfect as possible. As perfect as possible—not perfect—because there are no perfect jobs.

I have found that it is difficult for most people to stay motivated on any one job for more than five to seven years. The human being is built to be challenged—to be stretched—to learn new things. Those who are not challenged every five to seven years encounter the *glide slope*. Performance starts to slip just a tad—until over a period of years performance has slipped to an unacceptable level. Then we wonder what's happened to Ole' Joe or Ole' Jane. Well, they're just sick and tired of doing the same thing for 25 years. They're counting the days to retirement, not yet recognizing that a person has to do something worthwhile until he or she dies. And maybe even after death—I don't know about that yet.

A job change every five to seven years? Definitely—and you've always heard that people don't like change. (If the word *change* spooks your people, don't use that term. Everybody loves *opportunity*. And they love *improvement*. After all, if a change isn't an improvement, we're not going to make it.)

I can prove without a single thread of doubt that people love change. I've tried this with hundreds and probably thousands of people through the years. The results have always been the same.

"OK, you don't like change," I tell our employees. "If you don't like change, I'll double your present income and give you a written contract to work your present job—in exactly its present form—until you retire when you're 65 years old. If you're unable to do it, you have to give the money back with interest."

I've never yet had a taker. Then I extend the stakes—a salary of $100,000 a year; $200,000 a year; $300,000 a year; $400,000 a year; $500,000 a year.

In a group of about 300 people recently, I got one hand at $500,000 a year. Then I asked the rest of the group, "Do you think she can do it?" The audience responded with a resounding *noooooo!*

Obviously, I wouldn't offer this to 64 year olds. I tell those in this age group that they're ineligible to participate.

You see, if people don't want to do the same thing until they retire—and if they don't like change—what else is there?

This proves, I believe, that people like change. What they don't like is for change to be crammed down their throats. They like to have some input into the situation. They need to be told of the reasons for the change—what happens to them in the process—how they will be affected if it doesn't work out. Lay all the facts on the table. And take your time in making the change. Most changes we make in an organization are not life and death matters if they are not fully accomplished by tomorrow morning.

This gets back to excellent communication—the primary job of the leader.

A friend of mine who recently retired as the CEO of a competing company was always in the process of reorganizing his company. I often chided him that he centralized in the even years and decentralized in the odd years. Obviously my accusation was an exaggeration, but I think I learned something about the management process by watching his company from a distance. His company was in constant turmoil. People were being moved around often—from city to city—as one office closed and another absorbed the work. Yes, the constant reshuffling provided an opportunity for him to stimulate his people—to get the right people in the right slot. People were challenged frequently. Ineffective people were not offered jobs after the reorganization. No one had an opportunity to become overly comfortable in any one slot.

Perhaps his method worked. But I think families of the employees were subject to stress and shock that for the most part were unnecessary—and the cost to relocate the people was enormous. I prefer, first, to hire good people who have the ability to move upward in an organization and to accept new job challenges through the years. We'll talk more about hiring later.

One way to provide job stimulation is to post every job opening, with an explanation of job requirements, salary range, and every detail of the job. Anyone who thinks he or she can handle the job should be encouraged to apply for the opening. Those who apply should be interviewed for the job, as would be the case with an outsider.

Some managers don't want good workers to leave their departments, but it's much better that they leave a department and go elsewhere in the company than leave and go to a competitor—or worse, go into the glide slope and become ineffective employees after several years.

Employees also need to know what's going on in the company, and they need to understand the significance of the role they are playing in the success of the company. There must be some fulfillment from their employment. They must be able to see progress on a day-to-day basis.

New opportunities. Improvements. New challenges. Job fulfillment. These are the ingredients of the *near perfect job*.

SILVER BULLETS

▲ Employees—both old and new—seek out the perfect job.

▲ Few can define that perfect job—because there is no such thing.

▲ It's difficult for most employees to stay motivated in one job for more than five to seven years. Human beings are meant to be challenged.

▲ People *love* change—because they love opportunities and love improvements. What they don't like is having change crammed down their throats.

▲ Post all job openings to create challenging opportunities.

▲ New opportunities—improvements—challenges. These are the ingredients of the *near perfect job*.

The Magic of Motivation

20

SO MONEY MOTIVATES?

What motivates people? Probably 95% of the people I speak to answer *money*. Perhaps money plays a role in motivation—but money by itself does not motivate.

If money is a motivator, professional athletes earnings millions of dollars a year would always be motivated. But they're not. They need motivation just like the rest of us. Entertainers earning millions of dollars a year become depressed just as often—and probably more often, it seems—than those of us struggling financially from payday to payday.

You have heard for many years that we attract good people by paying attractive salaries. That's true too. But paying more than a job is worth can be a dissatisfier, not a satisfier. "Amateur" managers often make this mistake. Thinking that they buy the respect and friendship of their subordinates, they often attempt to pay more than jobs are worth.

Doing that is not healthy for the company, is not healthy for employees, does not make the manager more popular with employees, and does not buy more respect for the manager. Nobody wins.

You may recall the days when Eastern Airlines was still in business. Just prior to folding their tent, the baggage handlers were on strike. According to published reports, the handlers were making about $45,000 a year—and that was several years ago when that was a lot more money than it is today. Those folks didn't like their jobs. They were bored. They felt they were in dead-end jobs. Yet they couldn't leave because they could not come close to matching their Eastern salaries anyplace else. Frankly, their baggage handling skills put to work elsewhere would have been worth about one-third of their salaries at Eastern Airlines. The employees were in jail—they had no place else to go.

Let's say you have a file clerk earning $25,000 a year—well paid in today's values for the skills required for that job. He has excellent filing skills—so good that you would like him to stay with your company until his retirement in some 40 years. You increase his salary to $100,000 to make sure he stays.

Will the $100,000 salary make this file clerk happier? Perhaps for a few weeks—but only a few weeks. (Remember the professional athlete who makes several million dollars a year?) This person will become an unhappy, unchallenged, disgruntled employee who has no alternative but to stay in this job for the remainder of his career—another employee in jail. Unhappy, unchallenged employees tend to pull co-workers down to their level.

Morale problems are often associated with overpaid jobs.

Bored, unhappy employees—employees who don't like their bosses, don't like the industry, don't like the company, the hours, the location, or the benefits—should be able to leave your organization, go elsewhere, and make about the same amount of money by using those same skills.

Last week I talked to a vice president of a very large company who was making an exceptional amount of money. He is looking for another opportunity for the remaining 15 years or so of his career before retirement. Why? "I'm bored," he said. "I'm working about two hours a day." A doubling of his very substantial salary wouldn't change this person's attitude toward his job. A person can't cut down a tree with an ax handle, no matter what the pay is.

Don't misunderstand my point. Employees should be able to earn more money. Every job should have a salary range that properly compensates the employee for the skills required to perform that job. New employees with little or no experience should enter the job at the bottom of the range, and the salary should move upward in that range as the skills increase and job performance improves. But that's what the job is worth. Never pay beyond the range established for the job.

More important, salaries should increase as an employee moves from Job A to Job B, requiring greater job skills and with a higher salary range. Then the person performing Job B should move to Job C, and from Job C to Job D. This individual will remain challenged and is much more likely to remain a happy, productive employee.

Someone once said that happiness is a pursuit, not a destination. Motivation is a pursuit, not a destination.

SILVER BULLETS

▲ Money by itself does not motivate.

▲ Paying more than a job is worth can be a dissatisfier, not a satisfier.

▲ Unhappy, unchallenged employees tend to pull co-workers down to their level.

▲ Morale problems are often associated with overpaid jobs.

▲ Employees should be able to earn more money by moving up in the salary range as skills increase and job performance improves.

▲ Salaries should increase as an employee moves from Job A to Job B.

▲ Motivation involves the pursuit, not a destination.

21
LIFE AFTER WORK

"Do you believe in reincarnation," someone reportedly asked a company president several years ago.

"I sure do," he replied. "Just stand at the door at quitting time and watch them come to life."

And indeed they do. Unmotivated workers during the work day tend to become highly motivated as they leave the workplace and begin to give attention to their "other life"— the activities in which they are involved after work, the activities which they consider "fun" and for which they are not paid.

I know personally people who are involved with these "fun" activities: I know a man who is a gourmet cook; several run marathons; one man builds furniture that would pass as having come from the showroom of the city's most expensive furniture store; two people I know build houses; several rebuild antique and classic cars; I know three people who rebuild airplanes and when the job is complete they fly them—now that's confidence. The list is endless.

These jobs aren't easy. Yet these folks think they're "fun," or they provide "relaxation," or "give satisfaction." You will note that these after-work activities are the very same jobs that other people do for money in their regular jobs.

The only difference between those who are engaged in an activity for "fun" and those who do it for a living is that those in the second group get paid and somebody tells them what to do. Think about this. You may be able to discover the secret of motivating employees in virtually any job.

The process of management—the very process that is supposed to bring about motivation—tends to destroy it. To turn the demotivated employee into a highly motivated one falls squarely on the shoulders of those of us called managers.

SILVER BULLETS

▲ Many employees "come to life" when they leave the work place.

▲ In many cases "fun" after-work activities are the same jobs that other people do for a living.

▲ The process of management—the very process that is supposed to bring about motivation—tends to destroy it.

22

FIRST AND TEN
The World's Greatest Motivation Technique

It's Saturday afternoon. You're attending a football game at your alma mater. Ninety thousand people are screaming—most are standing—bands are playing—cheerleaders are screaming—the score is tied. Your team has possession of the ball on the opponent's 30 yard line. Less than a minute remains in the game. Every eye is on the field—it's anybody's game. Enthusiasm is bursting the seams of the stadium.

Maybe we can't expect excitement and enthusiasm to be shown on the job as it is at this game. But wouldn't it be great if our people could get just half as excited about their jobs? Maybe there's a way.

Let's imagine that the rules of football are changed. After all, the rules of football are sometimes unfair. It isn't particularly unusual for one team to gain more yards rushing than its opponent, more yards passing, more first downs, more passes completed, yet fall short in the most important statistic—the final score. Shouldn't this injustice be rectified?

Under the new rules the white lines are removed from the field. There is no scoreboard, and there are no first down markers. Instead, the new system involves a sophisticated computer analysis based upon the precision of the plays being run, the accuracy of the passes, and the quality of the hits. This will be a much fairer system of determining the better team.

The players, coaches and spectators are told that the winner of the game will be announced six or eight weeks later, once the computer analysis has been completed.

If these were the rules, how many people would play the game? And how many people would watch the game? Chances are that not many would show up—and it's doubtful that the game would attract national television audiences.

How many people would bowl if they couldn't see the pins fall?

The reason that the American people are in love with sports is that the sports arena is one of the few places in life where they are able to get *fast feedback* on what's going on. In sports events, the players and spectators know what the score is, where their team stands on the field, and what they have to do to win the game. People want and need *fast feedback*—the world's greatest motivational technique.

Obviously, to suggest that the rules of football be changed is a little silly. Yet this is precisely how many of us run our companies. Employees are expected to put in their time, perform a certain transaction or process over and over and over, without knowing what they are contributing to the overall success of the company and without knowing what progress, if any, is being made. There is no scoreboard. There are no down markers. There are no officials on the field marking progress. There is no feedback of any type except a manager who quips periodically, "You're getting paid, aren't you?"

As someone is leaving work tomorrow, ask this question: "What did you do today? Did you accomplish anything?"

Most will say something like, "Nope"—"Same old same old"— "Nothing"—"I don't know."

People require fast feedback. They need to feel that they are making a contribution to something worthwhile.

A while back, while speaking at the Chamber of Commerce annual meeting in Greer, South Carolina, I had an opportunity to tour the local BMW plant. The assembly line is shaped like a lower case e. The assembly process starts at the tail end of the e and is finished in the center—so that workers all along the line can see the beautiful finished car to which they contributed. That's positive feedback—unusual in an assembly line operation.

At our company we formed a number of what I called *two-person companies*. This probably violates the rules of economics, which call for categorizing types of work and assigning each category to people who are paid the least amount to perform a particular task. Under this theory I should not be typing this page on my PC, for you can be assured that others can do the job better than I can, and some might even earn less than I do.

It was this theory that brought about assembly lines in insurance companies as well as in most other industries. While this probably makes sense from an economic standpoint, it makes absolutely no sense at all from the standpoint of motivation of people and quality of work. Most assembly lines provide very little positive feedback.

In the two-person insurance company, two people perform everything—and I mean *every* task associated with producing and servicing commercial lines of insurance. One individual is the "outside" person who calls on insurance agents and is responsible for both profit and sales of commercial insurance. This involves making the call, inspecting the business of potential clients, quoting the premium, and handling other front-end activities. The "inside" person is the support person who handles renewals of policies, most routine policy changes, many price quotations, and other support functions. The two work as a team.

The system has worked great. Our people like it. Our agents like it. We haven't had the first complaint from anyone involved with the process. It is the optimum of employee empowerment, a term that has come into common usage in management circles long after we adopted the two-person company idea.

Our people like it because it provides the ownership and feedback most people need. They "own" this little company, which serves some 18–22 agencies. Effectiveness and progress can be seen on a day-by-day, week-by-week, month-by-month, and year-by-year basis. No individual is lost in the machinery of an assembly line. Members of the team get feedback from the agency customers they serve. By getting positive feedback most of the time, it's easier for them to accept the negative feedback that will occur occasionally when they mess up something. On the other hand, when a person is buried in an assembly line operation, there is little feedback except when senior management gets complaint calls. Seldom does a customer call management with compliments. Thus, management feedback tends to involve negative situations.

Our agency customers like the system because they receive better quality work. Good people do even better work when they are totally responsible for their output. And agents like the relationship they build with their own two-person team. Customers—and the American people in general—are screaming for personal relationships. This is something that too many businesses overlook in their quest for efficiency. When a member of the two-person team leaves—and we encourage this under our theory that a person can't do the same job for more than five to seven years—half the relationship remains in effect, because it's unlikely that both members of the two-member team would move elsewhere within the company at the same time.

There is one downside of the two-person company, but I believe the downside is worth it. It's harder to replace good team members. In the old assembly-line days, we hired people at lower income levels, we assigned a menial task to that individual, training required a matter of minutes, and, in effect, we told them not to think, not to ask questions, "just do this little job until I tell you differently."

And we wondered why people were unmotivated and became sick and tired of those crummy dead-end jobs. There was no challenge; no one understood what role they played in the product and service we provided; and there was no urgency associated with getting the job done, not to mention getting it done right.

There's another advantage to the elimination of the assembly line. People make errors—and this will always be the case, no matter how well trained, no matter how intelligent, no matter how careful they are. In our business we found that a good, capable employee will make an error on about two percent of the transactions he or she handles.

If five employees in an office assembly line are involved in the process—and each of those persons has an error ratio of two percent—the compounded error ratio is in excess of 10%. In the eyes of the customer, an error ratio of two percent is bad enough; an error ratio of 10%+ is totally unacceptable.

Every now and then someone suggests we go back to the days of the assembly lines "because we can hire someone to handle certain activities for less." Doing so, however, would eliminate the dimension of "ownership" that is essential if people are to be motivated in their jobs. Quality would take a step backward. Customer service would likely suffer ("I don't know where the transaction is—I sent it to the rating department"). And the challenge of the job would be removed.

If you can come up with a system in which every worker is given *fast feedback* regarding the work that is performed, you'll have a highly motivated workforce.

SILVER BULLETS

▲ The American people are in love with sports because the sports arena is one of the few places in life where they are able to get *fast feedback*.

▲ The BMW assembly line is designed in such a way that workers can see the finished product come off the line—one way of providing fast feedback.

▲ Most assembly lines provide little positive feedback. This resulted in our *two-person company* concept in which a two-person team performs all activities regarding the sale and servicing of business.

▲ When more people are involved in a transaction, more errors occur.

▲ Fast feedback regarding the work that is performed will produce a highly motivated workforce.

23
YOU ARE IMPORTANT

A few days ago while eating breakfast at a Perkins Restaurant, I noticed a plaque listing The Employee of the Month. The unusual thing about this plaque was that over the past 10 or 12 months no employee's name was repeated.

I have trouble believing this. Most likely the best employee this month was also the best employee last month. And the best employee this month will probably be the best employee next month. Good employees tend to be good employees now and forever.

I've known situations where good employees have slacked off because of the heat they're taking from their cohorts. They don't want to be embarrassed again by showing up their fellow workers. So management tends to pass around the award to average workers who are able to walk, talk, breathe, and show up for work.

Lots of companies do this. Many have a special parking place for the Employee of the Month—when actually this employee and nobody else should have an assigned place.

This is the first rule of recognition: *The winner should not be limited to one employee.*

Let's say we're having a sales contest for a twelve-month period. Six months into the contest, one sales person is running 30% or 50% ahead of the rest of us. Those of us who feel we don't have a chance to win start slowing down even more—and making excuses—"because I didn't really try this year. My spouse was sick. We were looking for a college for our son. We moved to a new house." I can think of a hundred reasons that I didn't win—can't you?

*Recognition should be extended to **anybody and everybody** who makes it over the bar—not to just the **first** person over the bar.*

Many forms of recognition have been used at our company. I believe the following two programs have been most effective in creating a new corporate culture where employees think like owners, in building high morale and in developing a fantastic team spirit.

1. QUALITY PERFORMANCE BONUS (QPB)

"Wait a minute! I thought you said that money doesn't motivate. Now you're talking about motivating with money. What gives?"

Money doesn't motivate if it's viewed as an entitlement—if it's considered a given by the employee, such as the excessive salary we talked about earlier.

On the other hand, money can motivate if it is earned by achieving certain specific objectives. Those objectives must be carefully defined, not too complicated, very measurable, and always objective. The more frequent the payoff, the more effective the motivation.

The QPB is a profit-sharing plan paid to every employee company-wide on a quarterly basis. First, there is a trigger—the company overall must be profitable. Once that profitability trigger is reached, the bonus program goes into effect.

The bonus is paid to every employee in each profit center (such as a branch or regional office) as a percentage of base salary. Seventy percent of the bonus is based on that office's own profit picture, and 30% is based on the company-wide profit picture. For instance, if one office is hit by a hail storm and has no profit, but the company overall did pretty well, that office's QPB will be based on the 30% attributed to the company-wide profit figure.

This bonus has averaged 10% of each employee's base pay over the past several years, but personnel in some offices have received up to 70% of their base pay, and 30% to 50% of base pay is not uncommon. Those departments that support all profit centers, such as accounting, information technology, and executive, get the corporate average.

Everybody's eye is on the bottom line throughout the quarter.

At one point, the QPB—a very positive program—started to generate negative vibes. It's strange how positive things can become negative.

My predecessor told me of a wealthy local man who felt sorry for a family that had experienced more than its share of financial difficulties. Every month he sent the family a check for $50—a generous sum in those days. This continued for several months and not once did the family extend its thanks or otherwise acknowledge the gift.

One day the man asked, "Is everything OK? Are you receiving my check? Is there anything I can do to help?"

"Well, yes—there is something you can do to help," the recipient of the gift answered. "Could you get your check to us a little earlier in the month?"

That's a true story—although it's hard to imagine. But it proves my point—anything viewed as an entitlement seldom is appreciated. That's when positives sometimes become negative.

Our company pays competitive salaries. We're always in the main-stream with other companies in our industry. So I suppose there is no obligation to pay bonuses to all employees in excess of the already competitive salaries. But we do—to share the company's success with those who create that success—and to help our people stay focused on the bottom line.

But at one point we started to get questions—even from several senior management people who should have known better. "Why should our employees be penalized because of a severe storm over which our people had no control?"

"So you believe we should take the storm losses out of the calculation?" I asked.

"That's right," I was told. "Take out the storm losses."

"What about that $5 million uninsured motorists loss? That didn't result from the actions of our people. Should we take that out too?" I asked.

"Yes, take that out too," our employee responded.

"The insurance commissioner in one of our major operating states not long ago arbitrarily rolled back rate levels in one line of insurance. That was certainly beyond our control. Should that come out too?" I continued my questioning.

By this time several people in our group were beginning to feel embarrassed by their request.

"Look," I said. "This is the nature of our business. Every industry experiences good times and bad times due to circumstances over which it has no control. There have been times when realtors cannot sell houses because of high interest rates. How hard they work is not necessarily an indication of their success. Automobile dealers experience bad times because of economic conditions or high fuel costs—again, conditions over which they have no control. So it is in nearly every type of business I can think of."

A similar problem emerged more recently when some employees thought that the QPB bonus was being miscalculated. Again we took an aggressive position, explaining first in great detail how the calculation was done, and once more we explained how this benefit was over and above the benefits provided by most competing companies. Management offered it voluntarily—and management can eliminate the benefit just as easily.

Managers were told to keep selling the QPB idea. If the bonus becomes a demotivator, it will be eliminated. If it is a motivator, it will be continued.

Most people, I believe, understood. Several years have passed since then, and the QPB is still providing a terrific motivator to employees. It's an advantage that employees of our competitors do not enjoy.

No matter how attractive the benefit, continual communication about that benefit is necessary. Otherwise a most attractive benefit that should have overwhelming motivational value can become an entitlement—and for some reason people tend to complain about entitlements.

We ask that the value of the benefits be emphasized in every issue of the company's employee publication—we explain that job security and opportunities in the future are direct by-products of company success. As obvious as this is, a constant stream of communication is necessary to drive it home.

Without aggressive communication, even very positive benefits can turn into negatives. And should a negative occur, take charge early before rumors and grumbling consume the organization.

Remember the story—"Could you get your check to us a little earlier in the month?"

2. EMPLOYEE STOCK PURCHASE PLAN (ESPP)

The second program that had a big impact on changing the culture of the company is the Employee Stock Purchase Plan. Under this plan an employee may contribute up to six percent of his or her salary to the purchase of company stock. The money is accumulated over a six-month period. At the end of that period, the stock is purchased at the then current market price or at the price at the beginning of the six-month period, whichever is less, minus a 15% company contribution.

More than 60% of our employees participate in this program. So at least 60% think like owners because they are owners. It helps, of course, when the stock performs well—which again drives home the need and desire of all employees to make the company perform well. It has worked. Since the company became a publicly owned corporation in 1991, it has produced an average annual investor return of more than 20%. From 1991 through 1997, the company was the 85th best performer on the NASDAQ exchange.

These two programs are the "big ones" that employees talk about and think about. These are ways to keep the focus on performance and to let everyone know they are important and appreciated for making this company one of the top performers in its industry.

SILVER BULLETS

▲ Recognition should be extended to anybody and everybody who makes it over the bar—not just the first person over the bar.

▲ Money doesn't motivate if it's viewed as an entitlement.

▲ Money *can* motivate if it's earned by achieving certain specific objectives.

▲ Even a positive program can become negative if it takes on a dimension of entitlement. Managers must continue to sell the benefits of the program.

▲ Stock ownership helps employees think like owners because they are owners.

24

AND YOU'RE STILL IMPORTANT

Recognition, recognition, recognition. You can't give too much of it if it's genuine and if it applies to everyone who objectively earns it.

The 401K program is a fantastic benefit. Under our program, the company makes a 58% match of the first six percent of the employee's contribution. That's not a bad return—better than anyone will get at the local Savings and Loan. I often tell our employees that if they aren't smart enough to participate in the 401K plan and the Stock Purchase Plan, they aren't smart enough to work here. (Only about 85% take advantage of the 401K and 65% participate in the stock purchase plan. Yes, you're right—some are not smart enough to work here.)

Despite the tremendous value of this program, the pension plan, and similar benefits, they provide only a small degree of sizzle compared to the QPB and Stock Purchase Plan.

401K plans are so common from company to company that they have taken on an entitlement dimension.

The same goes for the other very attractive benefits offered to our employees. No company in our industry can surpass them. Yet, for the most part, they're considered entitlements. The absence of them will demotivate; but the benefits themselves are not motivators.

Early in my career, only a few employers offered Major Medical, covering the huge medical expenditures above the basic plan. Prospective employees would ask if the company made this benefit available. At that time the plan was a motivator. Now everyone has it—and nobody asks.

Eastern Airlines was the first airline to offer food on its airplanes to encourage people to fly with Eastern. Soon other airlines offered the benefit. Was it a motivator? Perhaps initially—but no longer. How long has it been since you've heard anyone give lavish praise to airline food? Now the airlines are trying to figure out how to eliminate it. The leading edge advantage doesn't last long.

So benefits are demotivators if they're not offered. But legitimate recognition is always a fantastic motivator.

Our company branch and regional offices earn plaques for reaching their growth and profit objectives. And individuals can earn President's Circle Awards for achieving certain levels of growth and profit. This award resulted from a conversation I had with one of our field sales representatives in the parking lot of an insurance agency in Dayton, Ohio. My predecessor had given senior officers tiny company logo lapel pins several years earlier. Our field sales rep pointed to my pin and said, "How can I get one of those?"

"What would you do to get one of those?" I asked.

"I'll do anything," he responded.

By the time we arrived home the President's Circle Award was born. It consisted of the company logo pin with a circle around it. We had bronze, silver, and gold versions for first, second and third year achievers. After that we went to rings, and we added diamonds for exceptional performance during successive years. This was not an expensive program—about $7 each at that time for the bronze, silver, and gold pins.

At one point we had Underwriting Sweepsteaks (yes, sweep*steaks*) for each branch and regional office. When an office met its growth and profit objectives, I personally donned a chef's hat and grilled steaks for everyone in the office.

Every complimentary letter or phone call we receive about the performance of any employee is summarized and published monthly in our employee publications. It's hard to measure the impact of that program, but it's sure to have a positive value. Everyone knows that we like happy customers.

We have given gifts selected from catalogs to data entry operators and other clerical workers who have exceeded their reasonable expectations (these are specific measurements that we will discuss later).

Teams who exceed certain profit and growth objectives can earn a Caribbean cruise for themselves and their spouses.

I said earlier that the recognition must be genuine. Let's say I walk into a department and shake hands with and congratulate a member of the department at random. Unknowingly, I had extended recognition to a person who is a drag on the department and may be on probation pending termination (and everyone in the department knows it). If you are going to extend personal congratulations, make sure you know the players.

Recognition lets people know that they are valued members of the organization and that they are appreciated. These programs need not be expensive—but they must always be genuine and objective. Recognition works.

SILVER BULLETS

▲ A company can't provide too much recognition if it's genuine and if it applies to everyone who objectively earns it.

▲ The absence of benefit programs will demotivate; but the benefits themselves tend not to motivate.

▲ Recognition must be genuine. If you are going to extend personal congratulations, know the players.

▲ Recognition programs need not be expensive—but they must be genuine and objective.

25

DO YOU WANT TO BE A MILLIONAIRE?

In a magazine interview a few days ago, I was asked to name three things that an aspiring leader needs to learn.

"Could I make it four?" I asked.

Given assurance that I wouldn't be disqualified if I named four things, I listed these items: Learn to speak; learn to write; learn to set a positive example; and learn to care about people.

We've talked about the first three at some length—they're all about communication, the ingredient most important to the field of leadership. But a leader must legitimately care about people too.

I can't begin to guess how many retirement luncheons and dinners I have attended over the past 40 years. As I listened to the kind words and testimonials of the retirees' co-workers, I began to recognize that the role of the employer is much more than a provider of biweekly paychecks to buy food, shelter, and the other necessities of life. Employers provide the environment from which personal relationships emerge. Our employees play cards together, go out to eat together, go to movies together, and even go on vacations together. We provide the foundation for the social life of many of our people.

Many new people start dressing more professionally because of their association with others within our organization. Many see a greater need for self-improvement and further formal education when they get caught up in the learning environment that exists in our company. In many ways, we, as the employer, are a mentor, advisor, and even a parent.

This is why I have tried to instill within our people the need for savings. It's sad to say that many—perhaps most—of our people have not learned this prior to their joining us.

Retirement is one of those needs that must be funded by savings.

When folks talk of retirement—especially early retirement—I ask them if they remember how much they were making 30 years ago. Most can come close. Think about this yourself. You'll be shocked.

Back 30 years ago if someone had offered you 100% of your salary to retire, you would likely have jumped at it. Had you done so, how well would you be living today?

The person who retires at 60, 62, or 65—may well live for 30 more years. Probably, the same types of economic conditions that have occurred over the past 30 years or so will be repeated over the next 30 years. There will be high inflation years and low inflation years. How well will you be living 30 years from now? Will the salary that is adequate in today's terms be able to sustain an acceptable life style in 30 years?

No one expects payments from Social Security to keep pace with inflation—if the program exists at all when now-young workers retire. And qualified pension plans can't keep pace, if for no other reason than reduced contribution caps placed on pension plans by legislators who are fearful of helping those "rich" people with family incomes of over, say, $60,000.

Saving also teaches discipline—a prerequisite for success in so many ways. Discipline is a prerequisite to learning new things, meeting deadlines despite adversities that emerge, using time wisely, meeting the requirements of demanding jobs, and balancing home life and business life.

If we really care about our people, we must encourage them to save. I suggest that first they contribute 6% of their salaries to the 401K plan. With the company match, this is their best investment. If they can't afford to do it all at once, they should split each pay increase until the 6% contribution is achieved.

Then they should start investing in the company stock purchase plan. Again, if they can't do it all at once, they can build up to it as their salaries increase.

Certainly there are uncertainties with any investment. If the stock market goes south, our stock will go south with it. So we can't guarantee that any investment will perform in the future as it has in the past.

Yet, if history is an indication of the future, and if our people make our company perform as we know they have the ability to do, these programs will continue to be excellent investments in the future.

If our younger people invest 12% of their salaries in these programs—and leave that investment in place for the long term—with the company contribution to both programs, the odds are good that they will become millionaires or multi-millionaires by the time they retire. And, remember, they're going to need tons of money to fund a comfortable retirement.

"But I can't afford to save," many people have told me. I understand this concern. As young parents, Sylvia and I likewise struggled from payday to payday. Despite our struggle, however, we always saved half of every increase in pay I ever received. This was before the days of the 401K, which takes much of the pain out of saving.

To the "I can't afford to save" argument, I ask, "What would you do if I told you that the company is not performing well—that it's difficult to meet payroll—that we have no choice but to make across the board pay cuts? Therefore, beginning next pay period your pay will be cut 12%."

Most people would complain to their spouses and cuss the SOB who is cutting their salary. Some, maybe most, would look for another job. But I'll bet you could get by, and, after a while, you'll adjust your living standards to the reduced salary and won't notice it very much.

"I've got good news for you," I continue. "We're *not* cutting your salary by 12%. Now invest the cut you're not getting."

It's been very rewarding to have employees tell me that they have done as I suggested—"and we're living as well as before and haven't really noticed."

One insurance agent once told me that he was concerned about the wealth we were creating in our employee force. "You're creating a Microsoft Syndrome," he said, "in which people will become so rich that they'll want to retire when they're 29." At this point it's not a problem, and it's a risk that I'll happily accept.

I think it's important as leaders to provide good jobs for people— to create opportunities for better jobs during their active working years—and to provide a means for a comfortable and enjoyable retirement. It's another way to care about our people.

SILVER BULLETS

▲ Four things a new leader needs to learn—to speak, to write, to set a positive example, and to care about people.

▲ An employer is more than a provider of biweekly paychecks. The workplace is often the foundation for the social life of many people.

▲ A leader should instill within people the need to save. Retirement is one of those needs.

▲ Think back to what you made 30 years ago. This will provide a perspective of the value of today's retirement income 30 years from now.

▲ Saving also teaches discipline—a prerequisite for success in many other ways—such as discipline to learn, discipline to meet deadlines.

▲ Many feel they can't afford to save. But most can adjust their living standards and will hardly notice.

▲ Leaders provide good jobs, create opportunities for even better jobs, and provide a means for a comfortable and enjoyable retirement. It's another way to care about people.

Building the Team

26
GUILTY UNTIL PROVEN INNOCENT

My company does not discriminate—and has not discriminated. Yet we've had our share of problems with the Equal Employment Opportunity Commission (EEOC). It's not fun to deal with the EEOC. The EEOC's philosophy seems to be that the employer is guilty until proven innocent. That's not the way our legal system is supposed to work in this country, but somebody needs to tell the EEOC. There is something inherently wrong with a system in which a government agency considers itself an adversary of American business and whose success is based on the reward it is able to get for a complaining party, regardless of the merits of the situation.

Nevertheless, this is a challenge American businesses must face. And through the years we have learned how to deal with it. The best way to avoid any charge that might lead to an EEOC complaint is to *hire good people*.

I believe that virtually every EEOC-type complaint we have ever had was brought about by hiring a person who did not have the capability to move up in the organization and absorb new types of work that virtually every job now demands.

It's hard to second-guess our predecessors, but I would imagine that most hiring decisions were justified by telling ourselves, "This industry doesn't pay very much, so we can't expect a lot from the people we hire."

We recognized that an individual, after three to six months on the job, is not a top performer. He or she is marginal at best. But we don't feel the pressure to take corrective action for "this industry doesn't pay very much, so we can't expect very much."

Now we have a marginal worker at best. There is no possibility of promotion. Unless the job is eliminated by automation, this person will have no choice but to work the same old job year after year. There are no new challenges to keep this person motivated. When the "glide slope" sets in as this person becomes bored with the job, there's no room to glide. Performance becomes unacceptable.

The problem is further compounded by the need, in most industries, to become more competitive, to be more efficient, to serve customers even better. This means there is little room in today's economy for employees who do not have the ability to be very capable performers. It seems to me that this is the case in every business in every industry.

When the manager or supervisor starts pressuring the person to perform at a higher level, a discrimination charge is filed.

It's critical that the company do what is necessary to defend its position that it does not discriminate. Never "buy off" the charge because of the high cost of legal expenses. It's a good investment to spend whatever is necessary to win the case, regardless of legal costs, for a "buy off" breeds other charges of discrimination from employees who want some easy money from the "tooth fairy."

Today, I believe it's safe to say that EEOC cases have pretty well run their course in our company. Most C grade performers of years past have either retired or left the company. The folks we are hiring now are smart, ambitious, motivated, and willing and able to take on new challenges throughout their careers. Even in a near no-unemployment economy, we have been able to hire people so good that today I couldn't get a job here.

You can't build a winning organization without winning people, who have the ability to grow with the company and move up through the ranks. It's also a great way to steer clear of the EEOC people who think we're "guilty until proven innocent."

SILVER BULLETS

▲ The best way to avoid EEOC-type charges is to hire good people.

▲ The need for good people is compounded by the need, in most industries, to become more competitive, to be more efficient, and to serve customers better.

▲ Never "buy off" a discrimination charge. This breeds other charges of discrimination.

▲ You can't build a winning organization without winning people— who can grow with the company and move up through the ranks.

27

FIRST RATE PEOPLE HIRE
FIRST RATE PEOPLE

"First-rate people hire first-rate people, second-rate people hire third-rate people," said Leo Rosten, the noted author.

Hiring first-rate people is the key to building a great organization that gets great results. Of course, that's easier said than done. First, most of us didn't have an opportunity to put together our own team on day one. We inherited a team already in place. It's easy to figure out what to do with the D and F performers—terminate them. And we know what to do with the A and A+ performers—put them in key roles in our organization. The B, C and C- performers are a greater problem—train them, motivate them, and encourage them to move their performance to higher levels. A good leader will have success with some, but not all, of the people in this category.

Even if we could hire our entire team on day one, we would make some hiring mistakes.

I've talked to people who claim to be so perceptive of the human race that they seldom make hiring mistakes, but I think that claim compares to that of gamblers who say they "just broke even." Somebody didn't break even—somebody had to lose. Studies have shown that relying on the average interview to fill a job opening is only 7% more accurate than flipping a coin.

My batting average in hiring first-rate people is far from perfect. I've hired people I would bet my last dollar on, and they have disappointed me. On the other hand, I've had concerns about average performers who have grown to become some of our most valued employees.

Airplane travel has a couple of advantages (and only a couple as nearly as I can see). It provides an opportunity to catch up on reading and allows time to think about things that are gnawing at you. On one particular trip, I was thinking about the performance of an individual who was in a critical slot in our company and whom we clearly should not have hired. Minutes later, in my catch-up reading, I came across an article about a Japanese company that conducted a full day of interviews for each new candidate. Their results with this process were compelling.

When I got back to the company we put into place a cross-interview process. Following an interview and preliminary screening by HR, each applicant was to be interviewed by no fewer than five individuals (who received special interview training), three of whom were not in the hiring department.

This process cut our hiring mistakes by about 50%—from the 18 to 20% range to the 8 to 10% range. There were several reasons for this. The hiring department began to take the hiring process more seriously, since a number of others were involved. And when interviewers were all from the hiring department, the questions asked tended to be technical in nature.

Interviewers from the non-hiring department were more likely to concentrate on other attributes of the candidate—attitude, team spirit, value system, work ethic, and the like. Following the cross interviews, the hiring department made the final decision, but the hiring manager had the benefit of several viewpoints that have proved to be of great value.

Several years ago, at a seminar for insurance company CEOs, one speaker's topic was how he turned a company that had been nearly bankrupt into one of the most successful companies in the country. Following his introduction, he hesitated for a few seconds and paced back and forth across the front of the room (as if he hadn't really given much thought to his topic). Then he began his presentation with this sentence: "If you're going to turn around a failing company, the first thing you've got to do is get the sour asses out of your organization."

That's not always easy. To eliminate the misfits is difficult, expensive, and time consuming. So doesn't it make sense to spend whatever time is necessary to do the best possible job of selection? I doubt that it will ever be possible to have a workforce that is always happy, always enthusiastic, every day. We all have bad hair days now and then. But certainly members of management, who must work as a team to accomplish a mission, must be reasonably compatible. If there are "sour asses" on your management team, I would suggest, at the very least, moving them out of management. Put together a management team that enjoys working together and that gets satisfaction from making a company successful.

Incidentally, what do prospective employees think about all the fuss of cross-interviews? We have found, nearly without exception, that they are impressed. They feel good about being associated with a company that spends so much time with a candidate for employment. They feel special when they are selected from a number of good candidates by several interviewers. And the process permits them to learn more about the company and become acquainted with several managers. With the cross-interview process, everybody wins.

A first-rate leader always hires first-rate people. A second-rate leader, who is always worried about being shown up by good people, isn't a real leader. With a turnover rate of, say, 10%, you'll have an opportunity to hire a complete staff of first-rate people over a period of about seven years.

S I L V E R   B U L L E T S

▲ First-rate people hire first-rate people. Second-rate people hire third-rate people.

▲ Hiring first-rate people is the key to building a great organization.

▲ A cross-interview process can cut your hiring mistakes in half. This process involves no fewer than five interviews, with at least three of them outside the hiring department.

▲ Eliminating misfits is difficult, expensive, and time consuming. So, it makes sense to spend whatever time is necessary to select the right people.

▲ Even candidates for employees like the cross-interview system. Nearly without exception they're impressed.

▲ A first-rate leader hires first-rate people. A second-rate leader isn't a real leader.

28

THINGS NO ONE EVER TOLD YOU ABOUT HIRING

JOB DESCRIPTION INFLATION: As you'll soon see, I have an anti-job description bias. I know—that won't make the HR types happy. But I've never known anyone who is any good who has read a job description more than once. It's usually read when a person gets a new job.

A person who isn't any good may read it more often. This is the person who says, "I'm not going to do that—it's not in my job description."

But I suppose some kind of a description must be written down—to permit the job-posting program to work and to establish a fair, consistent salary range for each job. But these things tend to get out of hand. I call it job description inflation. By comparison to job description inflation, economic inflation is zero.

On one occasion I had three job descriptions on my desk—one for the boss in a department, one for the next level below, and another for the third level below. All looked like they described the most important jobs east of the Mississippi River. I took the three descriptions to one of our key officers and said, "Rank these three jobs. Who is most senior? Who is at the next level? And who is the junior ranking person?"

Like me, he didn't know.

A fancy job description may attract a few candidates to a job being filled, but, for the most part, employees don't care about the job description. They're disappointed when a job is oversold. They're certainly not going to be fooled for long, because they've got to show up and work this job every day for several years.

Even accurate job descriptions become obsolete very rapidly in our business—and probably yours as well. About every three years most job duties change dramatically.

When a job description is written, insist that "inflation" be kept out. Just write down simply what a person is expected to do on the job and to whom he or she reports. Then permit the candidate to talk to a person now in a similar position. These are the real experts.

By all means, don't spend too much time and money developing job descriptions. They are nearly worthless.

JOBS, NOT POSITIONS: We have jobs—and we have careers. But we don't have positions. To me a person in an "ivory tower" has a position. In successful companies, we all have jobs—that require sacrifice, example, vision, and hard work—darned hard work.

DON'T MOVE BACK HOME: As it turned out, our son, one of our daughters, a son-in-law and a daughter-in-law chose the insurance field for their life's work. I'm pleased that they chose to follow in their dad's footsteps, although I was totally surprised because we never talked about it during their days at home.

They work for competitors because of the nepotism policy that we put into place when I became president of the company in 1983. Under this policy an employee cannot work within the jurisdiction of a relative, although they can work elsewhere within the company.

I jokingly tell our agents that there are a few competitors I want them to take care of—just enough so that our kids won't move back home.

It can be argued that a nepotism policy will eliminate some good team members. I think this is the case with my own children. But I believe the disadvantages of nepotism far outweigh the advantages. Therefore, I believe that any sizeable company should have a nepotism policy.

Nobody can win when sons, daughters, or their spouses are employed by your organization. First, the managers and supervisors feel as if they are being managed from both ends—from the top and from the bottom. They think that Big Boss Mom or Dad is getting a play-by-play account of everything that happens in the department. Even when you tell the manager, "Treat my son (or daughter) like everyone else," it won't be done—it can't be done. And every worker in the department knows it. Think about it and you will agree.

If a son or daughter is average or below average, chances are the manager or supervisor will not take action quite as soon as he or she would do with someone else. And if a son or daughter is the best employee to emerge in the entire universe in the past three generations, the manager or supervisor will be criticized for promoting the son or daughter too soon. "I know why he (or she) was promoted," fellow employees will say. The leader will be criticized for playing favorites whether or not the charge has merit.

Finally, the self-esteem of the child is damaged. Was the success earned? Or did dad do it for me?

A friend of mine says there is a three-generation cycle to the inheritance process. One generation makes it—the next generation sits on it—and the following generation blows it. There are many exceptions to his three-generation rule, but I've seen lots of kids of successful parents who didn't set any records of building a family business. As a matter of fact, I've seen far too many cases in which the kids not only ruined a business but also ruined a family.

Workers will view a nepotism-free organization as a fairer one—where a person can succeed because of individual efforts. The pay-off is a happier, more motivated work force, which brings about a better bottom line.

It is said that there are two ways to get ahead in business—select the right parents, or get results. Hire the ones who can get results.

HOW TO FIRE A FRIEND: This is simple—never hire a friend. It doesn't work. It's probably even worse than hiring your kids.

Don't get me wrong. My employees are friends—*business* friends. But business friends are different than *social* friends. Our social events involving business associates are *business* social events—which are different from *social* social events. My wife and I don't drink, so you may think I'm not qualified to give this advice, but never drink at business social events. Leaders need to be able to make use of their full mental capabilities at business social events.

As a leader and manager, you need to be able to take action when necessary—sometimes dire action. Maybe termination. Don't mess up great personal friendships by bringing personal friends into your business.

THIS IS NOT BRAIN SURGERY: Most jobs in American business—even very senior jobs—do not require geniuses. Give me people with average intelligence—with above average desire—and above average attitudes.

One of our employees once gave me a little piece of granite on which these words are inscribed: "Real leaders are ordinary people with extraordinary determination."

"You'll like this," she said—and I do.

THE BAD RESUME: In my some 40 years in business, I've never read a bad resume. So why hire from a resume? The only way to know how a person will perform on a job is to observe how he or she is performing in the present job. I've never known a person who does not perform one job well but will perform better in a job requiring greater skills.

RESULTS, NOT FUNDING: Have you ever noticed how politicians and bureaucrats talk about funding—"We can't do this job because we don't have the funding." Business people talk about results. You can learn a lot about hiring new people by listening to the words they use.

SILVER BULLETS

▲ Job descriptions are read only once by good people—when they're hired. Don't spend too much time and money developing them.

▲ Be aware of "job description inflation." Employees are disappointed when a job is oversold—and they're not going to be fooled for long anyway.

▲ Hire people for jobs, not positions.

▲ Nobody wins by hiring sons, daughters, or their spouses. Workers will view a nepotism-free organization as a fairer one.

▲ Never hire a friend. It's probably worse than hiring your kids.

▲ Most jobs don't require geniuses. Hire people with average intelligence, above average desire, and above average attitudes.

▲ There are no bad resumes—so why hire from a resume?

▲ Politicians and bureaucrats talk about funding. Good people in business talk about results.

29
COUNT TO TEN

"Have we got a problem," one vice president said as he stormed into my office. Before I had a chance to ask the nature of the problem, he whirled around and left, saying, "Yes, I can count to ten."

Later in the day he returned, "Well, that problem wasn't as bad as I thought. Here's how we handled it," as he explained the nature of the problem and the solution he and his people had worked out.

A leader builds the team by letting people struggle with problems—by letting them hash them out together. When there's a tendency to dump the real tough ones in my lap, I ask, "Can you count to ten? Come up with ten possible alternatives, and then come back and let's discuss it." If you can think of ten alternatives to virtually any problem, chances are one will stand out as the clear solution.

Asking your people to count to ten is a great way to build people and to avoid letting them put the monkey on your back. It's a great way to build a team.

SILVER BULLETS

▲ Come up with ten possible solutions to a problem. Chances are one will stand out clearly as the best.

30
WHERE THERE'S SMOKE

It started nearly 20 years ago with dozens of complaints from employees. "I can't stand it here anymore," was a typical comment. "I like George in the adjoining cubicle. I like him as an individual, and I have respect for him as an insurance professional, but I simply can't stand his smoking. But please don't let him know that I have complained."

Non-smokers had begun to speak out about this very emotional issue. I was receiving four to six letters a month like this. Clearly something had to be done.

We made the decision to become a smoke-free company—one of the first in Central Ohio to do so.

But how do we deal with such a highly charged issue? Can we turn a 90-degree corner?

At that time we learned that only 15% of our employees smoked. Thus, the problem was somewhat smaller than we had thought initially. Still we felt we could not alienate even 15% of our workers.

So we put together an 18-month phase out program, and all phases were announced up front. Phase One – Smoking was not permitted in the rest rooms; a non-smoking area in the cafeteria was designated; and individual "smoke eater" devices were made available to smokers at a subsidized price.

Phase Two – No smoking in the building, but a smoking area was designated in a courtyard outside the buildings.

Phase Three – No smoking on the premises, inside or out.

The 18-month phase-out program was continuously communicated throughout the company, and nearly continuous smoking cessation programs were conducted by an outside organization.

I'm not a supporter of anything "free." Something free too often gives recipients the impression it has no value. So we made the smoking cessation programs a double-your-money-back deal. If the employee (or a member of his or her family) was smokeless 30 days after the completion of the smoking cessation program, we refunded the $40 fee. And if the employee was still smokeless in another five months (or six months after completion of the program), we provided a bonus of another $40.

The statistics gathered from this program were somewhat questionable, but we know we made a lot of progress. We're reasonably certain that the smoking population was cut in half.

The complaints from fellow employees stopped. And we didn't get much resistance from the smokers. Many smokers, as a matter of fact, said that they needed this encouragement to do something that they had been trying to do for a number of years.

A big bonus that we had not expected emerged from the program. At that time the cost of our health insurance plan was rising at the rate of about 20% a year. The plan was self-insured by our company but administered by a third party that gave us some excellent statistics.

One statistic produced a fairly clear perception—not clear facts as such, since it cannot be proved conclusively—that the new smoking policy was having a major impact on health insurance costs. Again, no pure facts, but a whale of a lot of evidence supported it.

These statistics suggested that the 15% of our employees who smoked were costing 50% of our health insurance costs, while the 85% who did not smoke cost the other 50%. The illnesses costing the big bucks tended to be those of the smokers—not always, but usually—such as emphysema, heart bypass surgery, cancer, etc.

So we embarked on another program. Our company no longer hires smokers (except in those states in which it is illegal to discriminate against users of "legal agricultural products"—a fancy way of saying tobacco).

Over the past several years, while health insurance costs have continued to skyrocket, our company's health insurance costs have remained relatively stable.

As we studied smoking and its effect on our workplace, it occurred to us that our smoke-free program produced still another bonus for our company. Those employees who had the personal discipline not to smoke—or who had the personal discipline to stop smoking—tended to be better employees.

The reason, in my view, is discipline. Those who have the discipline not to get hooked or those who have the discipline to give up the bad habit also have the discipline to learn new jobs, to get things done, to get bottom-line results. After all, personal discipline is one of the most important traits of outstanding team members.

Over the years, I've reached this conclusion: Where there's no smoke, there's fire—the fire of determination to make a business successful. This is something for leaders to think about.

SILVER BULLETS

▲ Deal with high-charged issues (like smoking) by phasing out over a period of time.

▲ "Free" programs often are viewed as having no value.

▲ Smokers are probably responsible for the preponderance of health insurance costs.

▲ People who have the discipline not to "get hooked" or who have the discipline to stop are more likely to have the discipline to learn new jobs and to get things done.

▲ Where there's no smoke, there's fire—the fire of determination to make a business successful.

31
POLITICS

I'm not talking here about the excruciating kind of politics that involves professional politicians—promises that no one expects to be kept, horrible campaigns for election or reelection, and so many others things that most of us detest about politics. I'm talking about office politics—very distressing in many cases and sometimes quite damaging.

On the farm where we live, we have three barn cats—Heidi, Tizzy, and Miss Bibs. All came by way of our county humane society. They all have a good home here, and they are all making worthwhile contributions to a mouse-free and rat-free farm environment. They are all doing their jobs well.

Heidi was the first adoptee. She was queen of the hill. She had the whole place to herself, and she liked it. We were asked to accept a second cat, and we thought Heidi might like to have a friend. So we agreed. Contessa made the Bailey farm her home. But the name Contessa was much too sophisticated for our farm, so we changed her name to Tizzy. As far as we know, she hasn't minded.

But Heidi didn't care that much for her friend. Heidi was clearly the boss and would fight, hiss, and chase Tizzy whenever she got into Heidi's territory. But over a period of six months or so, Tizzy won out and started to establish the rules. At that point Heidi stayed in her own assigned territory in the barn.

Then the humane society asked if we would accept a third cat. Having never met an animal we didn't like, we agreed to make a home for Miss Bibs—who took over and established the rules— immediately. Miss Bibs was clearly the boss now—and Heidi, the subordinate, cozied up to Miss Bibs from the start and started working for special perks. Now Miss Bibs and Heidi are bosom buddies, sleeping on the same carpet together and spending most of their time together. Tizzy now follows the rules and spends time in her own assigned territory.

So it is in corporate politics (although I'm not suggesting that people sleep on the same carpet together). Especially as companies become larger, it's easy to see supervisors and managers start to align themselves with the person whom they believe has the inside track for advancement to the top job. Little political parties begin to emerge. It's Joe's people versus Jill's people. The emphasis is on a personal agenda instead of a corporate agenda.

If Joe wins out, his supporters rejoice. If Jill wins out, Joe's people start dusting off resumes and looking for new jobs because they had bet their money (worse than that, their careers) on the wrong horse. I've had dozens of calls from senior officers of other companies who have said that their careers have ended because they were considered one of "Joe's people."

This type of petty corporate politics is so bad in some companies that I don't see how they can get anything done It takes every ounce of human energy of every member of the team to make a company successful. There must be total cooperation. Everybody must march in the same direction and pull on the same rope. This is not possible when efforts are diluted by corporate politics.

I made it a practice to split up any corporate political party that I saw being formed. When one person started to build personal loyalty rather than company loyalty, that individual was going to get transferred to another slot where, at the very least, his or her political supporters would not be going along.

One officer was so blatant about attempting to align himself with the person he thought had the inside track that I called him in one day and said, "You can't figure it out, can you?" I thought that question would require a more thorough explanation, but he knew what I was talking about.

"No," he said, "I can't. And I've been wrong in trying to do so."

"You have talent," I continued, "but we're not getting full value for that talent because you're too concerned about building a secure future by aligning yourself with one person. Your skills will produce much greater dividends—for your career and for the company—if you align yourself with the mission of the company and not the mission of an individual."

There's room for only one political agenda at our company. That's the company's agenda. Everybody must support that agenda; everybody must work for its success; everybody must make significant contributions.

That's the way great teams are built and successful companies are created.

SILVER BULLETS

▲ When companies become larger, supervisors and managers often align themselves with the person whom they believe has the inside track for advancement. Emphasis is often on a personal agenda rather than the corporate agenda.

▲ It takes every ounce of human energy of every member of the team to make a company successful. There must be total cooperation—everyone must march in the same direction. This is not possible when efforts are diluted by corporate politics.

▲ There is room for only one political agenda—the company's agenda.

32

STRESS? I WOULD HOPE SO

There's much concern expressed these days about stress-related disabilities. When someone tells me that his or her job is stressful, I respond, "I hope so. It would be a boring job if it didn't present some stress."

I don't mean to downplay entirely the significance of stress, for there are some legitimate stress-related physical disabilities. But I would say that there can be more stress resulting from too little challenge on the job than from too much challenge on the job.

When people don't have challenge—or stress—on the job, they tend to find it away from the workplace, by doing everything from skydiving to bungee jumping or motorcycle racing. The same people who complain about job-related stress drive hundreds of miles, and spend a lot of money, to kayak on the most difficult white water river or play golf on the most difficult course.

To me, golf creates stress—I don't like to shoot 90 or 100—which is why I gave it up many years ago. Despite rumors to the contrary, I'm not anti-golf. It's just that I personally find it stressful. I don't even mind if people play "business golf" if it's truly for the benefit of business. And I encourage recreation. What I complain about occasionally is that some of us confuse "business golf" with recreation.

I also object to instances in which golf is a "good ole' boy" sport. The males in the company go to the golf outings while the females stay back at the office, turn out the work, and become infuriated because they're carrying more than their fair share of the workload. For them, that's stress. If the golf outing is supposed to create goodwill, it should do so. The outing should not create ill will for half the office staff.

Certainly, when a person complains of a stress-related ailment, by all means give it attention. Psychologists are available to deal with such problems.

But the best way to deal with stress is to hire the right people. People who want to learn, to accept new challenges, to rise in the organization to contribute to a winning organization, are seldom affected by stress. The stress or challenge of a task propels them to new heights.

The importance of selecting the right people can't be over-emphasized. It has become extremely difficult to eliminate ineffective people from an organization. There are more and more instances in which the employer is required to pay workers' compensation claims for employees who are taken ill while engaged in non-work-related activities, such as suffering a heart attack, allegedly because of stress on the job, while mowing the lawn on Sunday afternoon.

You're right. Selecting the right people is a stressful activity.

SILVER BULLETS

▲ Stress can result from too little challenge on the job rather than too much challenge on the job.

▲ When people don't have challenge or stress on the job, they tend to find it away from the workplace.

▲ When a person complains of a stress-related ailment, by all means give it attention.

▲ The best way to deal with stress is to hire the right people. People who want to learn, to accept new challenges, to rise in the organization, to contribute to a winning organization are seldom affected by stress. The stress or challenge of a task propels them to new heights.

33

THREE STRIKES AND YOU'RE OUT

Performance appraisals are frustrating. When every comment is positive, employees like them. When some comments are negative, employees are often resentful and hostile—and the managers doing the appraisals feel just as uncomfortable as the employees.

So what do we do? We tend to give glowing performance appraisals whether or not they are deserved. After all, this is what our mothers taught us—"If you can't say something nice, don't say it." All the performance appraisal workshops in the universe can't overcome the basic "be nice" principles that our mothers hammered into us so well.

I'm not opposed to "be nice" performance appraisals. Positive comments motivate people more than negative comments, and I believe in motivation. If there are areas that need minor improvements, tell the employee orally rather than in writing. Words on paper often are so cold that they can create emotional undercurrents that dampen the employees' self-esteem to the point that they are left gasping for air.

But there are times when negatives should be written down and acknowledged by the employee. I can think of several occasions when a manager decided that an employee must be terminated, but a review of recent performance appraisals revealed nothing that implied that the person was not the most capable employee that the company had been fortunate enough to hire over the last two decades. I've talked to employees right after their terminations, and I'm convinced that they legitimately did not know that their jobs were in jeopardy.

Couple this with EEOC challenges, and you have a recipe for disaster.

When there are performance problems, I like to see the "three strikes and you're out" performance appraisal. It goes something like this:

"Joe, you have some good qualities, and here they are. But there is a severe problem too, and here it is. As a matter of fact, you simply have to make progress in this area or we will be required to take *more severe action*. Let's review it in three months and see how you're progressing." That's strike one.

In three months, go through the process again. "Joe, you simply haven't made progress in the area we talked about last quarter. I want to emphasize the seriousness of this matter and to let you know that we're going to give you another three months to work on your performance. If we do not see appreciable progress, we have *no alternative but to terminate*." That's strike two.

Three months later there's another review. "Joe, we've talked about the seriousness of this problem over the last six months, and we still haven't seen adequate progress. Therefore, we must *terminate* your employment with us on this date." That's strike three.

Joe should have had no doubt during this period that he was in trouble—serious trouble—and that his job was on the line. He will not be able to say, "Nobody told me that I wasn't doing my job well."

Great leaders are continual communicators, teachers, and motivators. For them, the appraisal system is a continuing process, not a written report prepared once a year because the HR department requires it. The leader guides, strengthens, corrects, and teaches every day, always building a stronger team. When this is done on an ongoing basis, seldom are critical performance appraisals necessary.

On one occasion a junior officer was unhappy with me and became fairly belligerent. As I recall, he told me to stick it in my ear. Or, on second thought, it may have been someplace else.

I sort of lucked into a response. I looked sternly at him and said firmly, "Let's talk about this at 3:00 p.m. tomorrow."

As it turned out, the next 24 hours were agony for him. He imagined the worst possible outcome. There was more self-punishment involved than I could have possibly dealt out.

Our meeting the next day went like this, in cool, calm tones—something that would not have been possible a day earlier: "Bill, what happened yesterday was very much unlike you. You are normally a very cooperative, hard working individual—a team player—someone who really contributes to the success of the company. What's bothering you?"

By this time rationalization had set in. I don't recall the specific problem he outlined, but his reason was along this line—a family problem, the kids had been sick, he had a fight with his wife, he was just getting over the flu. He was most remorseful.

I continued, "I'm sure you know how important it is to all of us that we do everything possible to get the job done—with harmonious relationships with those we work with. Please don't let this happen again. I don't want you to risk your future career opportunities and job security at this company."

Had we tried to solve the problem when it occurred, I would have won. But the junior officer could have only lost. It would have been virtually impossible to resolve the matter to the satisfaction of both parties.

Of course, if it happens the second time, termination is in order.

By handling first offenders 24 hours later, there's a good chance to salvage what is otherwise a good employee while providing reasonable protection for that person's self esteem.

Oh, yes. What happened to the junior officer? He has continued to develop as a capable person and a significant contributor to the company. It never happened again.

SILVER BULLETS

▲ Performance appraisals tend to be positive, as taught by our mothers—"If you can't say something nice, don't say it."

▲ There are times when negatives should be written down and acknowledged by the employee.

▲ When there are performance problems, consider the "three strikes and you're out" approach—the first conference calls for improvement or *more severe action* will be required; the second calls for improvement or we have *no alternative but to terminate*; and the third calls for *termination*.

▲ A leader guides, strengthens, corrects and teaches every day, always building a stronger team. For a leader, the appraisal system is a continuing process.

SECTION VIII
A Penny Saved

34
FUN AND GAMES

For those of us who have been bitten by the business bug, business is fun. It's fun to sell products and services. It's great to see happy customers. Doing fancy new things with computers is fun. It's fun to build new buildings, buy new furniture, drive new company cars, fly on the company jet, eat good food at business luncheons and dinners, go to business conventions at exotic places, and associate with nice people. Business is really fun.

There's an essential ingredient of business, however, that's not so much fun. Most of us don't do it very well, and many companies that seem to have everything going for them fail because of it. That essential ingredient is *expense control*.

In virtually any industry, the companies that survive are those that are able to deliver great products and overwhelming service to customers very, very efficiently.

The leader has to get, and keep, a handle on expenses—even the modest ones. When I became responsible for our company, our expense ratio was considerably higher than the norm in our industry (about 35% higher)—so high that the company would not have survived. We went after the big dollars first—and that didn't take long because there are not that many big-ticket items. Then it was a matter of starting on the smaller categories of expenses that mount up fast.

We produced a monthly listing of all checks written during the month. It was quite a list—probably two to three inches thick. I didn't look at all the items, but I looked at enough of them that our people thought I looked at all of them. I sent dozens—even hundreds—of little handwritten notes—"What is this?"

One vice president took exception to an expense that I thought was wasteful. "It's only $2,500," he said.

"What would happen if I stood at the window and dropped 2,500 one dollar bills out on Broad Street?" I asked. "This would make the front page of the *Columbus Dispatch* tomorrow morning if not the national press. What's the difference?"

He agreed that there was no difference. Very soon this vice president was controlling the expenses of his department as well as anybody in the company.

Maybe this was a little dramatic. Maybe it was overkill. But these are the kinds of things a leader has to do, at least initially, to build a new culture and to establish a new value system in a company.

The ratios for various expense categories are published for all the companies in our industry—a highly regulated one. In non-regulated industries, public corporations file detailed information with the SEC, which makes the information readily available on the Internet. Find three to five of your most respected and efficient competitors—learn from public sources everything possible about them. Compare your company's expenses in every conceivable category with those of the competitors. Establish expense targets for every expense category and put together a plan to match or beat the expense ratio of your most efficient competitor.

You'll be told time and again, "It's just not possible to take that much off our expenses. We've already cut everything to the bone."

Your response is, "I know it can be done, because Companies X and Y are doing it."

But it cannot be done quickly. It will take months or even years. Establish an expense control goal of reducing expenses by, say, a half point a year. This will be an ongoing process, for you can bet that your strongest competitors have a program to reduce expenses. It's a moving target. Once you think you've arrived, you'll find that your competitors haven't been sitting still.

Prepare and distribute monthly reports on expenses, just like monthly sales reports. In staff meetings, place as much emphasis on expenses as on the other dimensions of the business. Let everybody know that expense control is as important as sales and other critical activities of the company.

There are many ways to control expenses—and most are relatively painless once everyone understands the seriousness of the matter.

SILVER BULLETS

▲ Expense control is an essential ingredient of business. It's not as much fun as some other business activities, but it's just as important.

▲ Compare your company's expenses to those of three to five of your most respected and efficient competitors. Set out to match or beat the expense ratio of your most efficient competitor.

▲ In virtually any industry, the companies that survive are delivering great products and services to customers very efficiently.

35

DON'T SPEND COMPANY MONEY LIKE YOUR OWN

"We're doing a great job of expense control in our company," it is often said. "All of us spend company money like it's our own."

That's a bad idea. The successful company has to do a lot better than that, for most of us don't do a very good job of managing our personal money.

I didn't fully understand this until we took our company public in 1991. At one of our 7:00 a.m. staff meetings, I told our senior people, "We can't expect the public to invest in us if we do not invest in ourselves. Therefore, all of us must make significant investments in our company."

"How much should we invest?" someone asked.

"I suppose it will vary depending upon your financial circumstances, but it seems to me that it must be a bleeding interest. All of us have to bleed a little if this doesn't work," I answered.

Now, these were senior officers of a major company. Most had had attractive salaries through the years. They all drove nice cars, lived in beautiful homes, and some belonged to prestigious clubs. They were pictures of the American dream. Several had accumulated significant wealth. Yet several others could not have come up with a few thousand dollars cash if their lives had depended on it. Their credit cards were at their limits; they had no significant balances in their bank accounts; they had "lived up" their salaries to the fullest. Now those people come to work every day to run multi-million dollar departments. We are supposed to take great comfort in being told that they "always spend company money like their own?"

I'm not critical of their spending their money in any way they choose. I don't want others to tell me how I should spend my money, and we shouldn't be telling them how to spend their money. But an expense control program has to be more carefully conceived than telling people to "spend company money like your own."

There must be guidelines. And those guidelines are set forth in a system we call *variable budgeting*. This is not a term you'll find in accounting textbooks, but the system works.

The variable budgeting process starts out with an estimate of anticipated sales for the new year. Then we determine the percentage of that gross income that can be spent for all expenses—*every* expense, including payroll, benefits, taxes, rent, and utilities. When the budgets come in high, we send them back for revision. If branch offices or departments perform similar activities, the expenses of those branches or departments are compared. Which is most efficient? We use the budget for that office or department as the goal for the others.

If the budget isn't approved by January 1 (or the beginning of the fiscal year), it's not the end of the world. Keep trimming until you reach your objective. There have been years in which we did not have an approved budget until May or June.

If anticipated sales goals are met, our expenses are at an appropriate percentage of gross income. Victory? Not quite yet.

By the end of the first quarter of the year, let's say sales are running behind goal; instead of growth of 15%, our growth rate is 12%. This is where the *variable* part of the expense budgeting process comes in. When sales for the new year fall below the mark for which we are shooting, expenses must be cut proportionately.

If one office or department has total expenses of, say, 2.345% of gross revenue, that office or department is expected to keep expenses at no more than 2.345% of gross revenue. No department's expenses can be permitted to exceed the fixed percentage agreed upon in the variable budgeting process.

Tough to do? You bet. But great leaders have great self-discipline— and great leaders spend money responsibly. With great discipline you'll find a way to keep expenses at the required level.

SILVER BULLETS

▲ Don't be satisfied when employees tell you, "I spend company money like my own," because many don't spend it wisely.

▲ There must be guidelines for spending—such as the variable budgeting system.

▲ When gross income falls below the anticipated level, expenses must be cut proportionately.

▲ Great leaders have great self-discipline—and great leaders spend money responsibly.

36
SIMPLE MATH

Every time I pick up a newspaper and read that 2,000 employees just got fired by a company somewhere, I bleed a little for them and their families. Most of these folks are probably good, honest, hard-working people who had committed themselves to doing a good job for their employer. For the most part they deserve better. Although there are exceptions, most are victims of poor leadership.

You see, management just didn't go to work some Monday morning and discover that the company was 2,000 people overstaffed. Very likely it had been overstaffed for months, maybe years. The conditions that led to the layoffs had been creeping up for a long time. It didn't just happen over the past weekend.

Why not vow this very day to make a commitment to do your utmost to take care of your employees? I've made this commitment to hundreds of employees for many years, and it has never had an adverse effect on the company: Employees are told, "You take care of the company, and we'll take care of you—is that a fair deal?" Everyone seems to think that that's a fair trade.

Making such a commitment to employees is not a reckless management decision. Conversely, I believe I can show that it pays off—every time. I believe I can show that employee layoffs weaken the company, not strengthen it.

Let's say that a company has just announced that it intends to lay off 2,000 people to reduce expenses and become more competitive. Every employee in the company—except the boss who made the decision—will assume that he or she will be affected. That is a normal reaction since most of us think negatively in situations like this. On the day of the announcement, everyone company-wide starts to polish up his or her resume.

Those who are offered jobs between the time of the announcement and the time of the actual layoffs will probably cut and run—and *the good ones always go first.* Your company becomes weaker because those who have more difficulty getting jobs elsewhere remain.

The good ones who leave join competitors and take with them your goodwill, personal relationships with customers, and product knowledge. I've seen this happen hundreds of times. Your competitors get stronger while you become weaker.

The good employees who remain with your company during this period are so frightened that they are paralyzed—they're waiting for the shoe to drop—so they're not as productive and effective in their jobs as they would be normally.

There's a better way to handle this. That better way is to *make a commitment today that we will not overstaff.*

Such a commitment requires a senior management team that believes strongly in a "lean" corporate culture, because leanness requires constant lectures, constant attention to detail, and insistence on results. (Remember, most aspects of leadership fall under the banner of communication).

There may be a day when the politicians will try to pass a version of ADA (Americans With Disabilities Act) to prevent discrimination against obese corporations, but they haven't thought of it yet. In the meantime, no overstaffing. A lean corporation can serve all its constituencies better than a corporation that is too fat to waddle.

How do we get there from here? Step one: Freeze all additions and replacements effective immediately.

You'll be making exceptions to this rule, as we'll discuss later. But if your company has a turnover rate of, say, 10% or 12%, you'll cut significant numbers over the course of a year—at much less cost and much less risk than that involved with widespread layoffs.

When newspapers report on companies laying off 7% to 12% of their employees, it occurs to me that that's probably within the normal attrition range. By freezing replacement and additional employees, they could have avoided all the downside of layoff announcements.

Step two: We have to find a way to determine when additions and replacements are legitimately needed. This, incidentally, isn't easy.

Start with the ole' eyeball test. In your informal tours through the various departments, do people appear busy? Is there an intensity of purpose? OK, this is not really scientific, but you'll learn a lot and you'll get a good feel for the situation.

There was once a rumor that I stood at the door at starting time and quitting time to see who came in late or left early. The story is an exaggeration, but when I'm out walking around the company at any time during the day I always observe the people around me. I smile at them and speak to them. I apologize to them if I made them feel guilty.

I learned a lot from such observations. I noted that sloppy work hours tended to occur in some departments more than others. Therefore, this is either a management problem—or an over-staffing problem. If the employees have nothing to do, I would prefer that they be with their families. We shouldn't expect them to sit on their hands.

Try this little experiment and see if the results are the same as those I have observed dozens of times: Go to the various managers throughout your company and ask how many additional employees they will need the following year. Always, always, always, managers say they have to have more people. There's just no way they can get along without more people.

Therefore, the news that there will be no additional or replacement employees will not be greeted with wild enthusiastic acceptance. There will be groans and complaints for a while. Initially, we had a few instances of "political slowdown" (the phenomenon of politicians cutting the most visible services when voters turn down a tax increase). Some managers may try their version of political slowdown.

Step three: Make the procedure a little more scientific. We formed an "employment committee" that consisted of three or four key people, including myself, that reviewed every opening. Every additional or replacement employee had to be approved by this committee.

Once the addition or replacement is objectively justified, post the availability of the job throughout the company. When the job is filled through posting, go through the same process with the new vacancy. As the employment committee goes through this series of vacancies created by the one job opening, the odds are very good that somewhere along the line someone will not need to be replaced—eventually bringing the employment count down by one at the bottom line.

Is this micromanaging? Probably so, but we found that middle managers have more difficulty with proper staffing than any other single activity.

We required that each request for an additional employee be accompanied by detailed documentation. That documentation was based on simple math. Ask questions. Count transactions. How many of those transactions occur every day? Just how long does it take a competent person to complete one transaction? Never, ever justify a job based on dollars. I've been told a countless number of times, "This job used to handle $400,000 of premium volume, and now it's $800,000, so we need another person." But dollars don't take inflation into consideration—or transactions that have been simplified through automation. Furthermore, the one person handling $400,000 of premium volume may have had a part-time job with full-time pay.

We asked a team of good people who were actually performing the transactions to establish their own Reasonable Expectations (which they called REs) for the job. We used a six-hour day as the norm, recognizing that time must be taken out of the day for training, work assignments, going to the john, or just visiting now and then. Efficient use of a solid six-hour day will produce good results without the danger of the workplace becoming a sweatshop.

A team of good workers setting their own REs—the number of transactions a person should be able to complete in a normal work day—will set higher levels than you will. Yet they will be fair. Others will know the REs are achievable since their peers set them.

There have been literally hundreds of examples in which simple math has saved hundreds of thousands, even millions of dollars. I was told 15 years ago that our life insurance company could not handle one more transaction with present staff. But 15 years later, with the same size staff, that company was handling three times the number of transactions. Furthermore, it was giving better service to its policyholders and agents than it did 15 years ago.

The manager of the department that produced our agent and employee publications told us that there was no possible way to do even one more ounce of work without additions to the staff.

Ten years later, those publications have been continued, the new Intranet publications have been added, many additional marketing activities have been added—with even less staff. To get the idea across, we actually counted the number of articles in an average publication. Then we asked, "How long does it take to write one of these articles?" Obviously, some require more time than others, but we came up with an average time. These are facts, not opinions, that few can dispute.

Workers are happier when staffing is at the proper level. Busy people are happy people. Poor morale is more likely to be the result of overstaffing than understaffing. It simply isn't healthy for employees to sit around and worry about whether others are carrying their fair loads. Busy people feel good about the contributions they are making and more easily catch the "team spirit" that helps make companies successful.

In our industry, payroll is the second largest expense category. Insurance claims of policyholders and claimants is the biggest expense category. So if an insurance company wants to save money, it has to look at payroll.

If payroll is too high, are salary levels too high or are there too many people? Our objective is to keep salaries "in the mainstream" of those of our competition, so our emphasis is on proper staffing levels.

When we save one dollar of payroll, we save one additional dollar in associated expenses. For instance, for every dollar of payroll there are benefits of perhaps 30 to 40%. Add the cost of a desk, office space, a telephone, a personal computer, a parking place, office supplies, and so on. For every dozen employees or so, there's the cost of another supervisor. It's safe to say that there's a dollar of overhead for every dollar of payroll.

Maintaining a proper staff level is probably the single most important thing you can do to keep expense levels in line. Proper staffing is not complicated. It's common sense—and it's simple math.

And what a fantastic way to give your people the security of knowing that their jobs are not going to be discontinued.

SILVER BULLETS

▲ Most laid off employees are victims of poor leadership.

▲ The conditions that lead to overstaffing occur over a period of months or years.

▲ A commitment to take care of employees will not adversely affect the company.

▲ When layoffs are announced, most employees start looking for other employment—and the good ones leave first. They take with them your goodwill, personal relationships with customers, and much product knowledge.

▲ Keep staffing in line by freezing additions and replacements. An employment committee must approve exceptions, and those exceptions are made only after the need is justified by counting actual transactions.

▲ Once an exception is approved, the job opening is posted. The employment committee then reviews subsequent postings generated by the first posting. Sooner or later in the series of vacancies/postings, there will be one vacancy that doesn't need to be filled, bringing the employee count down by one.

▲ For each one dollar of payroll, there is an additional dollar of expense for benefits, office furniture, telephone, computer, parking place, etc.

▲ With proper staffing, you are giving your people the security of knowing that their jobs will not be discontinued.

37

CADENCE

Automation is supposed to save money. And it *can* save money—but usually it doesn't. Normally, after a big automation project is completed, the company has the expense of the automation as well as the payroll expense that existed prior to the automation project.

The culprit is cadence.

Let's say that because of new automation in several job activities, the work loads of Bob and Judy have been significantly reduced. They are your most loyal, hardest working, smartest, most dedicated workers in the entire company. Certainly you don't want to lay off such outstanding people.

Bob and Judy are told that, because of their skills, dedication, and loyalty, they will be kept on despite a 50% reduction in their respective workloads because of the automation. Consequently, next week Bob and Judy now have only a half-day's work to do instead of the full day's work they had performed previously.

In six or eight months, how long will it be taking Bob and Judy to do their half day's work? Right! All day.

Now, these folks are not lazy, dumb, undedicated, or disloyal. They're top of the line workers. They're as smart and dedicated as ever. Their work ethic is just as great. What has changed in Bob and Judy?

Very simply, the only change is in work cadence. The pace has slowed because of the absence of work to do.

Several months later, Bob becomes bored and leaves for another job. You inform Judy, "Bob is leaving the company next week. Therefore, next week we are bringing Bob's four hours of work over to you so that you'll have a full day's work to do."

Can Judy do it? Probably not. Her cadence has slowed to half her former pace.

A few years ago, I ran two or three miles regularly. But I stopped. Today, I can't run two or three miles. It's not because I'm lazy or don't want to. I can't. At least, not until I build myself back up to that point by stretching my ability through a regular exercise program.

So it goes in virtually every job.

Most automation projects don't cut job activity all at one time. The cuts are phased in—by state or region or product line. Workloads decline slowly. And worker cadence slows along with the workload decline.

After conversion to the new automated system is complete, there comes a day when you realize that the payroll in that department has not declined. The head count has not changed. You ask the manager for an explanation.

"Everyone is working just as hard as they were prior to completion of the automation project," you are told. And they may be, either because of a slower cadence, or because new procedures often are more time consuming for a while.

If you doubt that new procedures take longer to perform than the original ones for a period, try this exercise in which I promise to save you 50% of your time. Write your name as fast as you can. Now write it again and leave out every other letter. What happened? It probably required two, three or four times longer to write half as many letters. So it goes with job procedures. It takes a while for new timesaving procedures to pay off.

How do we keep payroll in line while the automation project is being developed? During the feasibility phase, you should estimate how many people will be impacted by the completed project. At that time—when the project is just beginning—get a commitment in writing from the managers and supervisors involved that staff will be reduced by a specific number by the completion date. They are expected to spread the reduced work load appropriately as normal attrition occurs, so that the departing employees need not be replaced. If turnover does not occur fast enough, they are asked to encourage their people to apply for other openings in the company when vacancies arise. If turnover occurs too fast, they are asked to fill those vacancies with temporary employees or by overtime.

By taking these actions, we have found that we can reduce the staff at about the same rate as the work load declines through automation.

Our objective is to justify the automation project with direct savings in payroll dollars. The overhead-cost savings and improved service to customers become bonuses.

Cadence works in other ways, often creating an entitlement situation. A new claims representative joined our company in an outlying office many years ago. Right away, he recognized that the office was overstaffed. He simply was not needed. He worried about it. He couldn't sleep. He was fearful of being "found out" and fired.

But, due to cadence, he soon adjusted to his new lifestyle. He normally finished his work by noon, went out for lunch, had a beer or two, and went home.

Then one day he was given a larger workload and was asked to stay for the afternoon. He became bitter because the company was intruding on "his" time.

Fortunately, this man ultimately understood the trap that he had fallen into and was able to overcome it. He was promoted several times and has become a valuable member of management.

People are happier and feel better about themselves when the cadence is faster. Busy people are happy people.

SILVER BULLETS

▲ Automation is supposed to save money—but usually it doesn't. The reason is cadence. The pace of work slows as work activity slows.

▲ During the feasibility study of an automation project, determine its impact on staffing—and get a commitment from supervisors to reduce staff accordingly during the period the project is being developed.

▲ Justify automation with direct payroll savings. Other overhead cost savings and better service to customers are bonuses.

38
THE GREAT DINOSAURS

People—the most valuable resource in any business. People—the greatest expense in most businesses. People—the source of most of our joys and the source of most of our disappointments and problems.

Leaders lead people. They challenge them and motivate them. And to say that people challenge the leader now and then is an understatement.

One of those challenges is the creation of bureaucracies. Line operations—the departments that actually perform the transactions that serve customers—are relatively easy to keep bureaucracy-free. Just count the transactions, as we have discussed.

The job is harder in staff departments—the departments that support the line operations. Much of the "back room" work occurs in staff departments. Bureaucracy can build rapidly there, becoming the home of hundreds and thousands of corporate dinosaurs.

Here's Joe, a nice guy, been around a long time, knows the technical end of our business, but can't get along with customers. The first thing we know Joe is in staff.

And there's Betty, nice person, been around a long time, knows the technical end of our business, but doesn't want to travel as required by her job. Betty ends up in staff. And so it goes.

Every time we have people who for some reason do not want to—or can't—perform some activity that is a part of their jobs, we ship them off to staff, which becomes as over-staffed, bureaucratic, and non-responsive as three federal agencies trying to use up last-year's budget.

Certainly staff is necessary. But staff is overhead. Keep it especially lean and responsive.

Staff should consist of a few of your very best creative and analytical people—not the misfits. And the need for staff people does not necessarily grow as the company grows. You'll have many battles with your own managerial people on this one, but stick to your guns. For instance, if sales increase from $100 million to $200 million, are more accountants required? No—no more effort is required to work with big numbers. In our business, rate filings with state insurance departments require the same effort regardless of premium volume. Most aspects of staff work are the same, regardless of sales volume.

Too many people in staff jobs and too much bureaucracy kill otherwise effective business organizations. And staff departments are the most difficult to keep in tow.

You can easily see that I'm a strong advocate of not overstaffing. "What do you do to cover illnesses, vacations, and unexpected turnover," I'm often asked. The answer is simple and not inconsistent with the position I've espoused: Always keep a few people in the pipeline. These people should be learning the business, working solid entry-level jobs and earmarked for upward movement in the company. They should be learning how to serve customers, because customers may never be shortchanged in the interest of efficiency.

People "in the pipeline" do not necessarily constitute bureaucracy. It's the future of your company—if they're learning, if they're serving customers, and if they're not hidden in some obscure staff department.

SILVER BULLETS

▲ The creation of bureaucracies is a challenge to leaders.

▲ Bureaucracy is especially a problem in staff departments.

▲ Staff is necessary, but staff is overhead. Keep it lean and responsive.

▲ Staff activities do not necessarily increase as the company grows.

▲ It's necessary to keep people "in the pipeline" to learn the business, working solid entry-level jobs, and earmarked for upward movement in the company—always serving customers.

39

THE ROAMING MERCEDES SALESMAN

You should have this rule in your company: Never let the Mercedes salesperson call on the users of company cars.

If the Mercedes salesperson is given free-run of your company, chances are that he or she will do a good job of convincing your people that they should be driving company-owned Mercedes. They would arrive at customers' offices in better moods because of the comfortable cars. The prestige of the Mercedes would help them make sales—after all, people like to do business with successful people. Self-esteem would improve, another contributor to successful sales. And the car is safer—the company has an obligation to provide the safest possible work environment for every employee. Right?

Sold! Your people are impressed to say the least. "What a great employer!" they think.

"How fortunate I am to be hooked up with a company willing to give me a Mercedes."

Everything goes well until management is asked to start paying $70,000 a copy for company cars. Then they hit the brakes. People are upset. Morale declines. After all, they had been given the impression that the company was going to buy each of them a Mercedes.

Sure, this is an exaggeration. Yet that's precisely what we had been doing throughout our company for every new gismo that came along. Salespeople had free run of the place. Our people saw nifty office equipment and software sporting every imaginable bell and whistle. Really neat. Little or no payback at the bottom line—but neat. Everyone had been sold by the time senior management found out about it. But we determined that the stuff couldn't be cost justified and had to say "no." The job could be done just as effectively with equipment priced 30% lower. The velvet headrest and racing stripe just weren't necessary.

And our people were upset. By allowing the salesperson widespread access to our people, we had given the impression that we would go along with whatever our people recommended.

It's OK to involve your people in evaluating equipment, software, etc.—but only after management decides that some new form of equipment is a good idea and can add value to the company. Then let your people select from several options that may be available—products that offer comparable advantages at competitive prices.

But when we pull the rug out from under the decisions that our people make—decisions they thought had the blessing of management—people are upset and morale plummets.

Salespeople should have access to management and only management. Once management has cost justified a purchase, then involve your people in selecting models, manufacturers, etc. Their involvement can keep management from making some mistakes (after all, they're the ones who will be using it). They'll feel complimented that their opinions are valued.

But their recommendations should not be ignored—which often must occur when salespeople have free run of the company.

SILVER BULLETS

▲ Salespeople should not have free run of the company.

▲ By allowing a salesperson wide access to employees, management gives the impression that it will go along with whatever employees recommend.

▲ Involve employees in evaluating equipment, software, etc., once management decides that the new equipment can be cost justified and will add value.

40
GET OFF THE ESCALATOR

An inflation psychology emerged back during the high inflation days. No matter what the price for a product or service, everyone expected the cost to be higher next year. And even more the following year.

Escalator clauses became commonplace in nearly every contract—leases, software contracts, janitorial service contracts . . .

Today, inflation is tame in all but a few areas in our economy, yet the inflation psychology remains, and escalator clauses continue as standard fare in most contracts.

Consider a policy of refusing to sign contracts or leases that contain an escalator clause. Or at the very least, insist that the percentage increase be reduced to a low single-digit level. For instance, when a lease expiration is approaching we have found that many landlords are willing to trade a lease extension for removal of the escalator clause. The landlord knows he has a good tenant—a tenant that takes care of the property and pays the rent on time. And he knows that the space may be vacant for months or even years should the tenant move to another location.

Software people are particularly notorious for wanting to increase license fees for software every year, often by double-digit amounts. Resist this. Also, there may be competing software available at a lower cost. In the software (and hardware) field, product improvements are developing so rapidly that it may be possible to move to another vendor, get a far better product, at even less cost.

Why are escalator clauses so widely overlooked? We all think that next year will be better. Our industry won't be as competitive next year. Next year sales will take off and expenses won't be a concern. Next year—well, that's so far away that it's not a concern at the moment.

But in reality the business environment will be more competitive than ever next year. Margins will be squeezed more tightly. The weak operators will be forced out more rapidly. There will be a need to operate the business more efficiently than ever.

Think that's an exaggeration? I'm willing to bet that it's not.

The sooner you start breaking the inflation psychology, the better your odds of facing the more competitive environment that's sure to come.

SILVER BULLETS

▲ An inflation psychology emerged during the high inflation days that brought about escalator clauses in most contracts.

▲ Consider a policy of refusing to sign contracts or leases that contain an escalator clause. At the very least, insist that the percentage increase be reduced to a low single-digit level.

▲ Software product improvements are developing so rapidly that it may be possible to get a better product at less cost from another vendor.

▲ We tend to overlook escalator clauses because we think costs will not be a concern next year. In reality, competition will be greater next year. Margins will be squeezed more, and the need to operate efficiently will be greater than ever.

41

IS THERE A BETTER WAY?

Just yesterday, I visited a company that didn't have a good year last year. While walking through the building, I noticed "secretary bloat." Everyone seemed to have a private secretary—some had two. But none of the secretaries appeared to be busy. They looked professional, were extremely courteous, and made visitors feel welcome by offering coffee or soft drinks. But they weren't busy.

The CEO of another company I visited recently had three executive secretaries. In our company—several times larger than this one—I shared one secretary with two other senior officers. Carolyn is a talented, very capable person and had no difficulty doing our work. This is especially true in the days of e-mail and handwritten notes in the margins of letters.

We didn't ask Carolyn to get coffee or to run personal errands. This is an abuse of position, in my opinion. She is a professional, and we attempted to treat her as such.

This is just one more area where money can be saved. Have only as many administrative assistants as are needed to perform professional duties. It's not a matter of prestige—it's a matter of how many does it take to do the work.

This book is on leadership. Yet we've spent considerable time on cutting expenses. Why? If you're going to be a leader, you have to have something to lead. I'm totally convinced that a disregard of responsible spending is the primary reason most companies are forced to lay off hundreds and thousands of employees—and the primary reason most companies go out of business.

The leader must question every dimension of the organization. Is there a better way? Start with the pick up, delivery, and distribution of mail; examine how business is entered into the computer, how the product is shipped, etc. Can the process be simplified? Simplification generally reduces costs.

Is there a way to avoid one or two stops along the way? Is it possible to adopt a "touch it once" policy so that there are no assembly lines that slow up service and increase the number of errors?

A leader looks at the entire process—questions everything—continues to challenge people to improve the operation and deliver your product or service more efficiently. Challenge yourself to save your own annual salary every week by making an improvement that will cut costs and improve customer service in one activity. This is not an unreasonable goal.

The efficient operators will survive. Those who are not efficient will not.

SILVER BULLETS

▲ Have only as many administrative assistants as are needed to perform professional duties. It's not a matter of prestige—it's a matter of how many does it take to do the work.

▲ A disregard of responsible spending is the primary reason most companies fail.

▲ Challenge yourself to save your own annual salary each week by making an improvement that will cut costs and improve customer service in one activity.

42

LOOK A GIFT HORSE IN THE MOUTH

Leadership is about communication. And good relationships contribute to good communication. So doesn't it make sense that anything that contributes to good relationships should be encouraged?

Good relationships should be encouraged as long as those relationships do not contribute to decisions that are not in the best interests of the company. Receiving significant gifts, for example, could build relationships but work against company interests.

Let's say a rental car company hosted our claim managers at the Indianapolis 500. Or a reinsurance company took the person responsible for purchasing reinsurance on a hunting trip to Montana. Perhaps an investment firm invited our investment people to play golf at one of the country's finest golf courses.

Would these activities interfere with the quality of decisions? Would the interests of the company be adversely affected?

I can't be sure. But if there's any possibility of an impropriety, the practice should be discouraged. That's why we placed a $50 limit on gifts received from vendors or suppliers with which our company does business. What's magic about $50? Nothing really. I can argue that the gift limit should be zero. But it's doubtful that a person's integrity can be bought for $50.

And $50 will cover the normal business lunch. Even then, we tell our people who were recipients of business lunches that they should buy lunch next time so the net value of business lunches is zero.

One time, I received a call from a reinsurer that had been trying to do business with our company for many years. They offered first class airline tickets for my wife and me to Carefree, Arizona, top of the line hotel accommodations, food for three days, and golf at one of Arizona's most beautiful golf courses—all free. I explained our $50 gift rule and said, "This sounds like it might be valued at slightly more than $50—maybe even $60 or $70." I expressed appreciation for the offer and declined.

Had I accepted, would there have been an obligation to do business with this company? Would this have clouded my judgment? Would this have been in the best interests of our company?

I can't answer any of those questions except to say that there's a chance that this would not have been in the best interests of our company. When that chance exists, a leader must decline. Even if I had been sufficiently principled to avoid letting the junket affect the soundness of my decision, chances are that you would still question the appropriateness of the gift if you were a stockholder of our company. You would have had some question about my being able to make decisions that are always in the best interests of the company.

Decisions must be based on merit—the quality of service and the cost of the service. Therefore a limitation on gifts to officers and employees is essential.

SILVER BULLETS

▲ Good relationships with vendors and other service providers should be encouraged as long as those relationships do not contribute to decisions that are not in the best interests of the company.

▲ Receiving significant gifts build relationships but work against company interests.

▲ Decisions must be based on merit—the quality of service and the cost of that service. Therefore, a limitation on gifts to officers and employees is essential.

43

COMPUTERS AND GARAGES

No matter how much computer power and technological sophistication you buy, it all will be insufficient and obsolete in three or four years. The old computer will have a trade-in value of zero, or more likely you'll have to pay somebody to haul it off.

I've learned that computers are like garages. The bigger they are the more junk you store in them.

There are high odds that this very day someone in your company is doing a feasibility study on purchasing or leasing a new computer. He or she will have hundreds of reasons why buying a new one is essential—response time is slow, the software will not be supported within five years, you can get more computer now for less money than you paid three years ago.

Computer people always want bigger machines, the latest technology, and more bells and whistles. And these requests are always accompanied by justification charts showing millions of instructions per second and other statistics that leave most of us in a fog.

Challenge your computer people to take other steps to increase computer response time. Can we extend capacity for one more year without sacrificing service to customers? Can we get a one-year savings windfall that will flow directly to the bottom line?

Start the effort by "cleaning out the garage."

SILVER BULLETS

▲ Computers are like garages. The bigger they are the more junk you store in them.

▲ Challenge your computer people to stretch the existing computer capabilities for one additional year, perhaps creating a one-year savings windfall.

Serving Customers

44
FAST FOOD, INSTANT EVERYTHING

Customers today want instant everything. They want fast food and instant coffee. Most of us become impatient when our computer response time stretches to two seconds. (Remember when we told our customers that we would call them back tomorrow *if* we can find the file?) We're annoyed when someone we call doesn't answer the phone after the first ring.

Doesn't it stand to reason, then, that our customers want the same thing? They want instant service—and they may want it at 3 a.m. on Sunday. Instant service—now!

It doesn't matter what the service standard is in your industry. It doesn't matter that "our service is as good as anybody else's service," a battle cry that I've heard thousands of times. They want service now. It's human nature.

One of our insurance agents in the Cincinnati area dropped by his office to pick up something at 11:00 p.m. Sunday. While he was there the phone rang, and he answered it. "Paul," the caller said, "I traded off the old Buick and got a new Cadillac. Would you make that change in my policy?"

Paul took the information and told his client that the transfer would be taken care of. On the way home Paul realized, "You know, he didn't say anything about my being there at eleven o'clock Sunday night. He expected me to be there."

People expect good service when *they* want it—not when it's convenient for us.

I'm sorry to say that not that many years ago the service "standard" in our industry was 30 days for endorsement and policy issuance. As we started to change the company culture, we heard time and again that we were "doing as well as anybody else."

Obviously, change was not going to be easy. We decided to tackle the issue piece-by-piece, beginning in the department that had the greatest service problems—commercial lines underwriting. In those days, the commercial lines were not automated to the extent of personal lines. Much rating and coding, performed by computer today, were manual processes.

I asked an officer, who reported directly to me, to help us improve service and change the culture. We started out by counting the transactions coming in and going out of the commercial-lines underwriting department. This was done after normal work hours, and only the two of us knew that this was going on. What we found told us much about human nature and about what we had to do to turn around service and attitudes.

We found that the work performed each day always kept us at the "industry standard" 30-days-turnaround time. For instance, on heavy days we found that each person in one unit had processed about five transactions per hour, or about 30 per day, allowing time for training, distribution of work, restroom breaks, etc.

By coincidence, the Christmas/New Year season occurred during the time we were counting transactions. In our business, very few new business transactions occur during the holiday season. Therefore, we had some very, very slow days—one day, only about 20 transactions arrived for processing. Even with a relatively full staff that day, only about 20 transactions were processed—total.

The pattern was becoming clear. Our people were performing only the work that had to be done to keep service at the 30-days-turn-around mark, the service level that had been accepted by our industry and our company as the norm.

When work fell more than 30 days behind, the pace quickened, or overtime was worked, to get the backlog back to the 30-day level.

This study gave us the basis for a system in which we established Reasonable Expectations for every job, with output determined by a team of workers who actually performed that particular activity. When one department was up and running with the new measurement system, we moved to another, and then another, until the system was operating in most departments of the company. In each department, a plan was developed to eliminate the backlog and to keep work current in the future.

Throughout the development and implementation of this new system, we talked about the need to give *instant* service to customers. Work coming in today must go out today. After all, we always do one day's work at a time. It's easier to do today's work today than last month's work today, because there are no service complaints or calls to check status. The message was repeated with great frequency—which is how corporate cultures are changed.

In the claims area, our policy was to give 24-hour service. One of our competitors began an advertising program announcing its intent to give two-hour service. We felt that at least we had to meet the service of that competitor—but our people resisted. "It just can't be done," we were told. During one of my branch office visits, the manager, not knowing that this had been a topic of discussion, told me of the two-hour claims service pledge this competitor was making.

"Yes, we're aware of it—and we'd like to try it in one office. Do you have any suggestions?" I asked.

"Let us try it," he volunteered.

Bingo! The plan was put into effect. It worked well, and once it had been proven in one office, the other offices readily accepted the idea.

Now, it's not two-hour service—it's instant service—24 hours a day, seven days a week. The transition to "instant" service was easier than it was from 24 hours to two hours. Once everyone understands the expectations, and once attitudes begin to change, the team members jump onboard rather quickly.

Most people will do what is expected of them. Therefore, the key is to establish appropriate service expectations and not to rely on tired, obsolete, and unacceptable industry or company norms.

SILVER BULLETS

▲ Customers want fast food, instant coffee, and instant service. It doesn't matter that "our service is as good as anybody else's service." Customers want service now.

▲ Workers normally provide "expected" service—which too often is an unacceptable industry service norm.

▲ A system must be developed that will produce instant service to customers. The message must be repeated with great frequency— which is how corporate cultures are changed.

▲ Most people will do what is expected of them. Therefore, the key is to establish appropriate service expectations and not to rely on unacceptable industry or company norms.

45

WHY SHOULD I BUY FROM YOU?

For those of us who get up at 5 a.m. and go to bed at 9:30 p.m., it's hard to appreciate that there is a lot going on after midnight.

A company that bills itself as the world's largest automobile dealership claims that 70% of its sales are made on Friday night, Saturday, and Sunday. That happens to be a time that most traditional companies are not open for business.

I got my start in the insurance business with a company headquartered in Fort Scott, Kansas. The insurance company was by far the largest employer in this town of about 10,000 people. It was located downtown, within two or three blocks of all the retail stores.

The insurance company's core office hours ended at 5:00 p.m. The local retail stores closed their doors at 5:00 p.m.

But insurance people, being the inconsiderate lot they are, actually made it into some of these stores a minute or two after five but before the front doors were locked and, heaven forbid, tried to buy something. The store employees were delayed from their normal 5:00 p.m. activities, like golf and *I Love Lucy* reruns.

To avoid the inconvenience brought about by inconsiderate customers, the stores started to close ten minutes before five.

This worked out well for a number of years—until Sam Walton came to town, purchased a few acres at the edge of town, and built a Wal-Mart store. This store was open until 10 or 11 p.m. every day, including Saturdays, Sundays, and holidays.

Today most of the stores along Fort Scott's Main Street no longer exist. Of those that remain, many are struggling—and cussing Sam Walton.

But Sam Walton didn't put them out of business. They did it to themselves because they were not serving the customer.

In my 45 years in this business, I've become acquainted with thousands of insurance agents. But I've never met an insurance agent who *said* that he or she is not giving great customer service. However, I know that some do not give great service because we receive requests from customers to be transferred to another agent because they felt they were not getting good service.

I often ask agents, "Why should I buy from you and don't just say 'great service;' spell it all out for me?" It's not a bad question for anyone in any business.

The American people are demanding *service*—overwhelming service. And this applies to every business in every industry. Maybe it's time to rethink what service really means.

Are you really providing it? Instantly? When the customer wants it?

SILVER BULLETS

▲ It's a 24/7 economy. Most cars are sold on Friday night, Saturday, and Sunday. People want to shop in the evenings and on weekends.

▲ "Why should I buy from you and don't use the word *service?*" is a good test.

▲ The American people are demanding service from every business in every industry.

▲ Rethink what service really means. Are you really providing it? Instantly? When the customer wants it?

46

FOR CUSTOMER SERVICE, PRESS 5

Throughout my career, I've answered my own phone. I have talked to claimants, to policy-holders, to agents, to salespeople, and to others whenever they called. It has not been overburdening to do so. Most people work through the channels and respect the time of the CEO. Taking such calls also permitted me to "feel the real pulse" of the company from time to time.

Customer service receives heavy emphasis in our company. After all, without customers, none of us are necessary. Yet still we receive complaints. We receive about two complaints out of every one thousand claims handled. I wish there weren't any complaints at all, but we have never been able to eliminate all of them. Under the best of circumstances, an insurance claim is an inherently negative experience, even though we try to make it as positive as possible.

Rate increases? Yes, we receive complaints—from both policyholders and agents. The rate-making process is relatively simple in the insurance business—many people pay the losses of the comparatively few. As the cost of lawsuits spiral, and as costs skyrocket for fixing more expensive automobiles, those increases are reflected in insurance prices. We always try to remain competitive in the industry, but, most important, we always give greater value than our competitors, which has kept rate complaints at a relatively low level.

But nothing in the company—I mean nothing—ever generated the number of complaints we received when phone mail started to phase in without proper guidelines.

After installation of a new phone system a number of years ago—the first time we had phone mail capabilities—phone mail just took off. We didn't guide it. Within days, my phone started to ring from irate agents and policyholders. "If you don't want to do business with me, just tell me so!" one caller screamed. Slam, as he hung up the phone. Then another—and another—and another similar call.

We set out to investigate. We found many of our people "hiding" behind phone mail. "I had a lot of things to do this morning," one underwriter told me, "so I put my phone on phone mail." We found that callers had to endure a series of menus as calls were bounced from phone to phone.

Many things in life are hard to understand. One of the most difficult is how strenuously our people defended the need to rely on phone mail even though they themselves became infuriated as they encountered "phone mail hell" when dealing with other businesses.

Certainly phone mail has its place in American business. I'm not opposed to phone mail for inside calls—that is, when one employee within the company calls another employee within the company.

But customers should be able to talk to real live human beings. I believe it is clear that in American business most people want to do business with people. This is a primary reason that the dot-coms of the world have become dot-bombs.

I believe that a customer should never experience more than one automated message before talking to a real live human being. The menu should be short—two or three choices max. Then, a human being should answer. At this point, if Mr. Smith is out, and the caller is willing to talk only to Mr. Smith, I have no objection if the caller is told, "Would you like to leave a message for Mr. Smith on his voice mail?"

This is far from a scientific survey, but I've asked several hundred people to name the most annoying thing about doing business with a specific company. Nine out of ten times the answer is the company's phone mail. Try this yourself. Of the companies you deal with in your personal or business life, what annoys you most?

Do you want to take a huge step to improve customer service and customer relations? Take a look at your phone mail system.

SILVER BULLETS

▲ Phone mail often generates more customer complaints than anything else.

▲ Phone mail has its place in American business, but it should not be overused. A customer should not experience more than one automated message before talking to a real live human being.

▲ Most people want to do business with people.

▲ A review of your phone mail system may be the single most important step you can take to improve customer service and customer relations.

47

THE 40-HOUR WEEK

It's fun to study successful people. Generally, there are discernable differences in patterns of behavior between successful people and those who are just getting by. Work hours provide one such pattern. I've never known anyone who made more than a basic living by working just 40 hours a week. Most very successful people take whatever time it takes to achieve success.

The core workweek in our company totals 37½ hours, which applies to those who are not exempt from wage and hour laws. Exempt employees, on the other hand, are expected to do what is necessary to serve their customers. HR manuals make no reference to work hours for exempt employees.

Do these high expectations work counter to our efforts to make our company a good place to work? I don't think so. I feel strongly that happy employees are those who have committed themselves to serving policyholder and agent customers. They get great satisfaction from, and want to be a part of, a worthwhile mission.

It's this worthwhile mission of giving overwhelming service to customers that caused us to discourage a full-blown flex-time policy under which employees could choose hours that best fitted their personal schedules. Customer service always comes first. That means that our people must be on duty when our customers need them.

Of course, special hours are a normal part of our operation. The mail and distribution department works two overlapping shifts— starting at 6:00 a.m. and ending late. Mail is to be on the desks of our employees by the beginning of normal core hours, and mail pick-up occurs after normal core hours. Computer operations are 24/7 activities. Likewise, the claim department is open for business 24/7. Line operations' hours vary by the time zones being served.

All these special hours are designed to serve policyholders and agents in the most prompt, efficient manner possible.

Does this conflict with the employees' needs for flexible work hours? Sometimes it's a balancing act. If all enterprises operated for the convenience of employees, restaurants would not serve food at normal mealtimes and ministers would not work on Sunday.

Although we have eliminated most "assembly line" operations, there are still some processes in which person A's work at 8:00 a.m. becomes person B's work at 9:00 a.m. If person A decides to come in at 9:30 and person B comes to work at 7:00, service to customers quickly deteriorates.

Good service to customers creates more success and more job opportunities. Therefore, the absence of full-blown flextime does not necessarily work to the detriment of employees.

We make every effort to be as considerate and compassionate with employees as possible. We always remain alert to their special needs. But no company can afford to let flexible work schedules adversely affect service. Customers always come first.

SILVER BULLETS

▲ No one makes more than a basic living by working just 40 hours a week.

▲ A key to success is: Be there when the customer wants service.

▲ Sometimes it's a balancing act to accommodate employees' needs for flexible hours without sacrificing service to customers.

A Million Little Things a Leader Has to Do

48
THE "BORED" OF DIRECTORS

Everybody has a boss—even the big boss has a boss. That boss is called the board of directors. One of the millions of little things a leader has to do is assemble a board that does what a board is supposed to do. And, let me tell you, that's no easy matter. A board nominating committee tends to create a Good Ole' Boys' Club, which is not necessarily in the best interests of the company.

Board members fall into four groups, and three of them are bad.

1. **Inside Directors** — The big boss often likes inside directors whose primary mission in life is to keep the big boss in office. But that's not the purpose of a board. This group is viewed as evil by investors, and it is probably true that an insider can provide no more counsel as a director than he or she can as a member of management. It's impossible for an insider to be a subordi-

nate 361 days a year and be a boss (a director) for four days a year. This group should be kept to a minimum.

2. **Bored of Directors** — These are the folks who seem to say, "Hurry and get this meeting over with so you can give me my director's fee and I can get out of here." This group won't hassle you, but they won't help you either. Of the boards on which I have served, these members constitute a majority.

3. **"Manager or Director?"** —— These people don't know the difference between the functions of management and the functions of directors. Some seem to be thinking, "I've always wanted to run a major corporation, and this is my chance."

I have seen boards that want to make virtually every management decision, including approval of every management change down into the mid-management and supervisory ranks. "Making people decisions is one of the hardest things I do and I observe people at least 250 days a year," I remind them. "It's not possible for you to make accurate judgment calls on people when you have an opportunity to observe them only a few hours a year." The leader has to be able to put together his or her team, not a team designated by the board.

Boards of directors cannot manage a company. They may have experience in other industries, but not yours. To manage a company competently, the leader must live with it 250 days a year if not 364 days a year (it's OK to take off one day a year without thinking and worrying about the company). A director cannot be an expert in your industry by being exposed to it a few days a year.

Individuals in this category cannot help your company perform. It's even possible that their intrusion will be damaging to the company in the future.

4. **Real Board Members** —— These are the directors who can be helpful. And, boy, are they hard to find.

They are independent, have no conflict of interest, can advise and counsel fairly, have no hidden agenda, and can give a different perspective to top management. This group should be looking at the big picture with you. If you start to get off course, their advice and guidance should bring you back to center. If the company is not performing up to par—or if the company is not operating within the guidelines the board establishes—their purpose is to fire you and bring in someone who will help the company reach its potential.

People like this are more valuable than any team of high-priced consultants. (I've found that most consultants are unemployed people with business cards.)

Convince your board nominating committee that we want *real* board members, not necessarily their buddies, friends, neighbors, relatives, bankers, or lawyers. Real board members are very valuable and are real bargains—management consultants that you don't have to pay as management consultants.

SILVER BULLETS

▲ Board members fall into four groups, and three of them are bad.

▲ Inside directors may keep the boss in office, but they can add no more value as directors than they can as members of management.

▲ The *bored* of directors is interested in the directors' fees, nothing else.

▲ Some boards don't understand the difference between board functions and management functions.

▲ *Real* board members are independent, have no conflict of interest, can advise and counsel fairly, have no hidden agenda, and can give a different perspective to management. These members are more valuable than consultants.

49
THE HEAD JANITOR

When I've been asked what I do for a living, my standard answer has been, "I work for an insurance company." If they drilled deeper, I'd say, "I'm the head janitor."

It's true. A leader really is the head janitor. The quality of food in a restaurant can be judged by the cleanliness of the windows, whether the grass is cut, and whether there is trash in the parking lot. They are symbols of management. If management is not meticulous about what customers *can* see, just imagine what conditions are like in the kitchen where customers *can't* see.

The same is true in any business. When a leader doesn't care about the appearance of the premises, I would doubt that the leader really cares that much about the quality of service to customers. The leader insists that the buildings and premises remain neat and clean.

Even senior management people too often believe that building cleanliness is "not my job." Remind them that the appearance of the premises is everybody's job.

The janitors in our company have a schedule. Certain stairways, for instance, are cleaned on Tuesdays and Thursdays; other stairways are cleaned on Mondays and Wednesdays. Other cleaning activities likewise occur on a schedule. I have my own Janitorial Quality Control test. Walking through the buildings was a part of my communications program—and walking the stairways was a part of my exercise program. When I noticed a small scrap of paper on the stairway, I would kick it up against the riser and take note of the day of the week. Then I would count the days it remained there. If it wasn't cleaned up promptly, I would know that the cleaning schedule is not being maintained.

About ten years ago, I was to make a speech at one of the Disney hotels in Florida. As an early riser, I woke up at about 5:00 a.m. even though my speech wasn't scheduled until 9:00 or 10:00. I went to the dining room at about 6:00 a.m. and found it didn't open until 7:00. So I picked up a newspaper and sat in the lobby until the restaurant opened.

Shortly after 6:00, two painters entered the lobby with buckets of white paint, paint trays, and rollers. They made a quick tour of the room and touched up every little scuff mark or scar. They had completed their mission in the lobby in less than five minutes and moved on. As I looked around it appeared that the building was brand new, with a totally fresh paint job.

When I arrived home, we put into effect what I called the Disney Maintenance Program. On a weekly schedule, our maintenance people tour each building and touch up marks on the paint. We've been doing this for ten years, and all the interior walls still look like the painting crew just left the building.

There are a number of advantages to such a program. It's more economical than having a crew come in and do a complete paint job, and employees are more careful about keeping clean walls scuff-free. Remember how it feels to put the first ding on your new car?

Clean and neat buildings and grounds are symbols of professionalism, build pride among employees, and impress customers and other outsiders. Where else can you get those big benefits for such a small investment?

Congratulations to the leader—the Head Janitor.

SILVER BULLETS

▲ The quality of food in a restaurant can be judged by the cleanliness of the windows, whether the grass is cut, and whether there is trash in the parking lot. It's a symbol of management.

▲ When a leader doesn't care about the appearance of the premises, it is doubtful the leader cares that much about the quality of service to customers.

▲ The buildings can look new all the time with a weekly touch-up program.

▲ Clean and neat buildings and grounds are symbols of professionalism, build pride among employees, and are impressive to customers—great value for a small investment.

50

A BORING STRATEGY

Our company has been successful partially because it has had what I've called *a boring strategy*. We've stayed right on track despite new fads that have come along and despite advice from many so-called experts. We've stayed with the business we know.

Without exception, companies that are successful know their business.

A number of years ago, there was a conglomerate movement in this country. Diversification was popular. Peter Lynch, in *One Up on Wall Street*, calls it *diworseification*.

In those conglomerate days, it was generally believed that a good manager could manage anything, whether or not the manager knew the business. Perhaps there are a few superstars who can do that, but it has been my experience that truly outstanding companies and excellent managers know their business.

Obviously, we must listen to our customers. As customers' needs change, the company must change. In many cases, however, it may be better to be a fast follower than a leader, introducing a new product or service after a competitor has made the bleeding-edge mistakes.

Will focus groups keep you on course? They may help, but always use common sense. Remember that nobody ever asked for a Walkman or a VCR. Technology drove the creation of those products rather than the product resulting from consumer demand.

When we introduced our non-standard automobile insurance product several years ago, we held agency focus groups throughout the first state of entry—Ohio. We met with dozens of agencies that had experience selling non-standard auto insurance for other companies. In every meeting, we were told that low-commission products were not wanted, were not needed, and would not be sold. We were told that we would waste our time, significant expense, and much effort if such products were introduced. Therefore, our people recommended to senior management that we introduce only a product that paid a standard commission.

"I don't feel comfortable with that, despite the recommendations of the focus groups," I said, "because they're selling low-commission products for our competitors."

We decided to offer both flavors of products, just in case— a standard-commission product and a low-commission product. Some 12 months later, we found that more than 65% of the sales were the lower commission product—a product that we were told was unneeded, unwanted, and would not be sold. Some ten years later the low-commission product still accounts for the preponderance of sales.

They were not expressing it in words, but here's what the focus groups were really saying: "I would *prefer* not to sell a low-commission product—unless the customer insists on the low-cost product."

A vast laboratory exists in virtually every business in America—the competitors. Competitors are constantly testing new ideas. They are continually involved in real-life research through market acceptance and rejection. Any real competitive advantage doesn't last long, because good ideas will be picked up quickly by competitors. Be in a position to fast follow—often a more practical approach than being on the bleeding edge.

Stick to what you know. It's impossible to be successful in a field in which management does not have expertise. Management must understand it, live it, and breathe it. What made a company successful will likely keep the company successful.

Go to school on your competitors. Let them make many of the expensive mistakes. If they can't make money with a certain product or service, chances are you can't either. If they can be successful, you can be more successful because you can avoid many of their gear-up costs, avoid most of their mistakes, and more likely be in a position to leap-frog ahead of them. The fast follower often is in a better position than the first company off the blocks.

SILVER BULLETS

▲ Companies that are successful know their business.

▲ Diversification is sometimes called diworseification.

▲ It may be better to be a fast follower than an innovator.

▲ Focus groups are sometimes misleading.

▲ A vast laboratory exists in every business—the competitors.

▲ Any real competitive advantage doesn't last long. Good ideas are picked up quickly by competitors.

51
NO R&D

I've already told you what I think of consultants (unemployed people with business cards). I have similar confidence in experts in consumer research. Most of the market research calls I get are from telemarketers who are reading a script and have about as much interest in my views about a product or service as they have in reading last month's *Wall Street Journal*.

There's a better way. We forego R—outside research—and get on with the D—product development. If the product doesn't work, we chalk the experience up to research.

Certainly, there is a need for homegrown research in our business. Pay attention to consumer needs; watch the activities of competitors; and examine new products that they introduce. In our heavily regulated industry, we can get copies of competitors' products, prices, etc., from state insurance departments.

We can talk to agents (whom we often share with those competitors) and get their views about the new product or service. We learn everything possible about it.

Then our product development team incorporates the strengths of competitors' offerings and avoids the weaknesses that our agents tell us about. Yes, there are gear-up costs, but often the gear-up costs are no greater than the cost of hiring a market researcher.

To the best of my knowledge, we were the first company to accept credit cards for payment of insurance premiums. A few months after we introduced the service, we received a call from a vice president of our bank asking for permission to give our name to a market research firm that had been hired by a competitor to study credit card payments. We learned from the market research people that they had been paid $250,000 to do the research—more than our costs to develop the concept.

Of course, we're not looking for a cure for cancer and are not seeking FDA approval. For companies like this, research is a different matter.

Many businesses, however, can save money and do more meaningful preparatory work by doing D, not R.

SILVER BULLETS

▲ It may be better to do D, but no R. Develop a product—D; if it doesn't work, call it research—R.

▲ Development costs are often no greater than the cost of paying for market research.

52
RUN AWAY FROM HOME

A friend and counterpart of mine recently retired from a competing insurance company. "I moved to Florida," he said, "even though I'm not that fond of it."

"Why did you move to Florida if you don't like it?" I asked. "I don't see anyone from the Florida Chamber of Commerce holding a gun to your head."

"I was so overly involved with community activities," he continued, "that I found I could not retire in this city. I had to run away from home."

As leaders, we want our companies to be good corporate citizens. Also, we individually want to do our share in paying back the communities that have meant so much to us.

But there's a saturation point. Leaders of significant companies can become so overly involved with community activities that they don't have time to lead their own companies—which is their primary mission. I've seen a number of companies get into financial difficulty because their leaders spent too much time away from their companies doing good deeds for their communities.

Yes, it's important to play an active role in one or two outside activities in which you have an intense interest. Another key officer can take part in one or two other outside activities in which he or she has a special interest. Another officer can participate in still other community activities. The company, therefore, is being a great corporate citizen by participation in a wide array of civic and charitable organizations.

I didn't recognize this initially, but I found that most of the boards on which I was asked to serve are "Give and Get" boards. My presence was wanted because of the money I would "give" personally and the money I could "get" from others. This can be a costly process, for the contributions game tends to be a tit-for-tat situation. For every $1,000 I was able to collect from other companies required a similar commitment when their CEOs came to me for requests to give to their favorite charities.

As a leader grows, time constraints become greater. It's important to be selective and limit outside activities to those whose missions you especially value. And retain an appropriate balance between inside and outside activities. Remember that your primary mission is to lead your company. Never put yourself into a position in which you will have to "run away from home" when you retire.

SILVER BULLETS

▲ A company can be a great corporate citizen by asking several top officers to participate in one or two civic or charitable causes in which they have an intense interest.

▲ Recognize that many boards are "give and get" boards. Your presence may be wanted because of the money you will "give" and the money you can "get" from others.

▲ Be selective—properly balance inside and outside activities—and keep primary focus on leading your company.

▲ Don't become so overly involved with civic and charitable activities that you have to "run away from home" when you retire.

53
SUE 'EM

Whenever there are business disputes with suppliers, customers, or others, someone nearly always suggests, "Let's sue 'em."

"I know who's going to win," I answer. "The lawyers. The lawyers on both sides will win and both the plaintiff and defendant will lose." I know a lawyer who claims he has never lost a case. "Now, about half my *clients* have lost their cases," he continues, "but I've never lost because I always got paid."

When there are disputes, try to work them out. Talk, talk, and talk—and see if you can find common ground. And don't be so hard-headed that you won't compromise. Do your best to settle. Sometimes compromise involves very insignificant points that really don't matter much. I joke with my colleagues that I'm always willing to compromise if we don't give up anything.

Lawyers charge an hourly rate (in 15 minute segments—or 10 minute segments if you're lucky). A telephone call, therefore, is considered 10 or 15 minutes. I've found that lawsuits develop something like this:

"We have a good chance of winning this," the lawyer says after he hears your side of the story.

Over the next 15 or 18 months the meter runs every time someone touches the file, a deposition is taken, or a phone call is made. We're talking real expense dollars.

Finally, a court date has been set. Days before the trial date, your lawyer says, "Maybe we'd better settle this. A lot of new information has been developed over the last 18 months. Some of our witnesses are not as good as we thought they were. They don't remember the facts as well as they once did. One of our best witnesses died. The odds are not really good that we can win."

So you compromise and settle—something you could have done 18 months ago without incurring tons of legal expenses.

Is there a time for lawsuits? Certainly. I believe that EEOC suits should be defended to the end, for it's critical that your company prove to the world that it does not discriminate. To settle an EEOC complaint may send a signal to others that they too can file a complaint and make easy money. When defending such complaints, however, use a lawyer who specializes in those matters.

Most people I've dealt with through the years are decent, hardworking, honest people—the salt of the earth. What they say is better than any contract any lawyer can write. In a business proposition, once the two of us agree, I write down each point in good old common English language—1, 2, 3, 4. Then we decide which party's lawyer will write the legal document—ours or theirs. If the other party's lawyer wants to do it, fine—let the other party incur the expense. Then we take the draft to our lawyer and say, "Please review this and tell me if there is anything here that will work to our disadvantage. Don't criticize form—just substance.

Just tell me what words in the document that should be changed to accomplish our mission."

When there are two or more sets of lawyers in the room at the same time, you can figure on a blockbuster bill. I've seen two sets of lawyers argue about one word for hours—when the word didn't really make any difference. It's often a matter of, "I like the words in my data processing system better than the words in your data processing system."

Am I entirely anti-lawyer? No. Lawyers have great value. Some of my best friends are lawyers (despite the lawyer stories I continue to tell them). Our general counsel at our company is one of our most valuable team members. Management people with legal backgrounds but who do not practice law are often among the best.

Keep the lawyer's role in mind. Your lawyer's purpose in life is to keep you out of trouble. "Here's what we want to do," I explain to our lawyer, or "Here's the contract we want to sign. What downside do you see?"

There are risks associated with anything. Do the upside gains far overshadow the downside risks? Even when odds are slim, are downside risks so great that the company might be put out of business? The lawyer can help you evaluate the risks—but you make the decision, since many lawyers are risk adverse.

SILVER BULLETS

▲ When there are business disputes, talk—don't sue.

▲ Yet lawyers can play a valuable role, such as evaluating risks involved with a business proposition.

54

WILL THE MEETING PLEASE COME TO ORDER?

Since leadership is virtually synonymous with communication, it seems inconsistent that I would say that the American business world has too many meetings that are conducted too poorly. But I believe that's the case. Too many meetings are held because it's time for the meeting, not because there are issues to discuss. And too many are held without appropriate time limits.

For more formal types of meetings, few leaders understand Roberts' Rules of Order. Farm kids in 4-H generally know Roberts' Rules. Outside of those with 4-H backgrounds, I don't see many leaders who understand how to conduct a formal meeting. Sooner or later, Roberts' Rules will get you out of a jam. You'll need to know how to amend a motion, how to amend the amendment, and how to restore order from chaos. If you don't know Roberts' Rules, learn them.

Of course, most meetings are not formal meetings, and with these the leader doesn't need to worry about Mr. Roberts. Yet, there should be an agenda (simply a list of one, two, or three issues that need to be discussed), and attendees need to be armed with the list and with homework assignments before the meeting.

Someone should take minutes—not necessarily formal minutes, but a summary of the topic or topics that were discussed, what conclusions were reached, who is responsible for taking the next step, and the date that next step is to be completed. Without minutes, someone is going to forget where things stand (some might not even know what conclusions were reached without that summary). Some will forget that "they've got the ball" or will forget the deadline. We are all busy people with lots of things on our plates—we have many excuses for forgetting. Without minutes, you'll find yourself covering some of the same ground at the next meeting.

Oh, yes. The females in the group don't always get hooked with the jobs of being the secretaries. If there is no formal officer structure in which someone has that specific secretarial responsibility, take turns.

And another thing: a time limit. Chances are you can get as much done in a one-hour meeting as you can in a meeting that lasts two or three hours. In so many cases, the work fits the time available.

Have respect for the time of the attendees—start the meeting on time. Let's say the meeting is billed to begin at 8:00 a.m. At the announced starting time, seven of the ten attendees are present, "but we'll wait a few minutes for the other three." You're wasting the time of the seven who were there promptly. At the next meeting, the same thing happens. Then, at the third meeting, probably a few more will be late, "because we never start on time anyway."

When the latecomers get there, don't go back over the first part of the meeting for their benefit. They can get filled in later—or they can wait for the published minutes. If they're in the dark a bit, they'll more likely be there on time in the future.

Is progress being made at the meeting? Just a few years ago, I was monitoring the progress of a data processing project (why am I always picking on data processing?) by reading the minutes of the meetings. There was a meeting on this issue, a meeting on that issue, and then another meeting on the first issue. In a one-page summary, there may have been references to ten meetings—but I never saw progress. When this occurs, the leader conducting the meetings needs guidance. Don't let the group wallow in frustration. Nothing can be more maddening than a poorly conducted meeting.

SILVER BULLETS

▲ For formal meetings, few leaders understand Roberts' Rules. Learn Roberts' Rules.

▲ Informal meetings should have agendas. The agenda and homework assignments should be distributed before the meeting.

▲ Take minutes—topics discussed, conclusions reached, who is responsible for the next steps, and the date the next steps are to be completed.

▲ Set time limits on meetings.

▲ Start meetings on time.

55

CAN YOU HEAR ME?

"I flew to Atlanta on a business trip last week," a friend told me, "and I heard some people at the airport talking about you."

"Was it complimentary?" I asked.

"Well," as he hesitated for a few seconds, "not really. It had something to do with computer software, and these folks were not all that happy with you."

I asked the date of his trip to Atlanta—and then checked my calendar. Now I knew who got caught with their mouths open at the airport. I might add, I wasn't entirely happy with the software company either, to say the least, but I didn't communicate it to the world at the airport.

We review this issue periodically at staff meetings: never, ever talk about customers when strangers might overhear. Never, ever talk about proprietary information when it might be overheard. A competitor might be willing to die for that information.

There's something about crowds at airports and in restaurants. It's as if these aren't real people, with spouses, and families, and friends—any of whom could be in your business. Perhaps it's a friend or next-door neighbor of the person you have put on probation and intend to terminate. Perhaps one is a sales person for your toughest competitor.

And cell phones. It's as if everyone thinks they're in an invisible glass phone booth where their conversations are entirely private. I've overheard sales people (how can you not overhear sales people?) talk about pricing a product—"If you have to go down to $279.95 a unit for Model X, go ahead and do it. And if Company Y—those jerks—come down too, take another $10 off that." Wouldn't Company Y love to know what the competition is up to? And they may know. An employee of Company Y may have been sitting at that very gate at that very minute.

"Can you hear me?" someone on a cell phone asks. "Yes, you are being heard. Everyone can hear you," I want to say.

Now this isn't really rocket science. But doesn't it make sense that top rate companies should not go around the country bad-mouthing their competitors or their customers or doing public performance evaluations of their employees?

At my company, our people are told to say kind things about our competitors outside the family—always. You can assume that every conversation will be overheard and that sensitive information may fall into the wrong hands. Personnel discussions are always private.

Incidentally, several days later I received a call from a vice president of the software company who had learned somehow that I knew about their conversation at the airport. "We owe you an apology," she said.

Obviously I knew the purpose of her call, but I asked, "Why do you owe me an apology?"

"We said some things at the airport we shouldn't have said," she answered.

"No apology is necessary," I insisted. "I like honest people—and I always like to know where I stand. I can take it."

Frankly, I wasn't that hurt by their comments. I'll always laugh about it. But I'll always have less respect for that company than I might otherwise have had.

My friend who overhead the conversation was likewise unimpressed, and others waiting for that flight weren't impressed either. "I hope our own people don't do that," they were probably all thinking.

Leaders lead in many ways—like reminding people that sensitive conversations and phone calls should be conducted privately. When it comes to communication, it's a small world.

SILVER BULLETS

▲ Never talk about customers or employees when it might be overheard.

▲ Proprietary information should likewise be guarded.

▲ Sensitive conversations and phone calls should be conducted privately.

56
WHO HAS THE BALL?

Several years ago we had a severe problem in one of one of the states in which we operate. We had fumbled every aspect of the matter badly.

"This is a serious enough matter that I think we should fire the person responsible," I said.

Every member of our senior staff group looked at me as they tried to figure out whether or not I was serious. Then I added, "Who are you going to fire?"

At that time we had a traditional organizational structure, with separate sales, underwriting, and claims departments, with staff departments supporting each of those functions.

Someone suggested we should fire the underwriter, another suggested the field sales rep, or the branch manager, and there were several other suggestions. At that point, everyone was beginning to understand my point—there was no clear accountability. Any person involved could easily point a finger at someone else.

Then someone said, "Since we're not sure who is responsible, it looks like it's going to have to be you." He was joking—I think.

In so many instances, problems have a splash-over effect, affecting many departments in the company. Few can be isolated to a single department.

Here's the test: When a problem arises, you should be able to call together your direct reports and ask, "Who is responsible for…"— name a problem. One hand should go up. If two or more hands go up—or no hands go up—or two, three or four individuals in the room say "kinda, sorta, maybe," you have an accountability problem. Your company will have difficulty negotiating the tight turns that most companies regularly encounter in today's business environment. You can bet such a company will perform poorly through the years.

Today, we're organized in such a way that there is clear accountability. It's easy to figure out who is responsible for a problem. Still, we believe it's helpful to thresh it out together—get all the facets of the matter on the table. Then ask, "Who has the ball?"

Before leaving the room, know who is responsible. "Cindy, you have the ball. Take the lead on this, you and your people come up with a solution, and report back to us next Monday morning." The specific report-back date should always be agreed upon.

Clear-cut accountability not only helps your company perform better, it also helps you identify the top performers who can be rewarded accordingly and given more important job assignments.

"Who has the ball?"

SILVER BULLETS

▲ "Who is responsible?" One hand should go up. If two or more hands go up—or no hands go up—you have an accountability problem.

▲ Conclude every meeting on any issue with the question, "Who has the ball?"

▲ Set the date when the person "with the ball" is to report back.

57

THE MORE THE MERRIER?

I have to admit, I'm not fond of committees. Two committees in our company work quite well. The employment committee approves additional and replacement employees. It is reasonably effective. The contributions committee is the most helpful to us. The committee allocates available monies to charitable causes—human services, education and the arts—and takes a lot of pressure off the CEO who is being hounded by a dozen community leaders daily to give to their favorite causes. Complying with all the requests for contributions to worthy causes could take the company to the edge of bankruptcy in a flash.

Beyond these two general areas, committees are helpful with regard to communication but are seldom helpful for making decisions and getting things done. I feel strongly that if you want to kill a project, committee it to death. There's an inverse relationship to the number of people involved with a project and the progress made with the development of that project.

Certainly many people need to provide input for a project, especially data processing related projects. Suggestion: call them teams, not committees. Perhaps there's not that much difference, but the term "team" has a connotation of action and results. That alone can't hurt anything.

Several years ago we had more than our share of problems arising from our IT Department, a fancy name for the data processing people. The newly developed IT projects were not being accepted by the users. Mistakes were rampant. Customers were having trouble understanding computer-prepared documents. I set out to find out why.

It didn't take long to figure it out. I found "committees" of 20, 30, or more people working on a project. At one committee meeting there would be perhaps 20 attendees. At the next meeting again there were 20 attendees—but many different ones than had attended the last meeting.

Somehow we had adopted "The More the Merrier" theory of project development. If ten is good, 20 is better, and 40 must be twice as good as 20.

After several years of losing money on our homeowners insurance line, my predecessor appointed a Homeowners Underwriting Taskforce to develop underwriting standards aimed at restoring profitability to that line. The group consisted of more than 30 people—and every one felt the need to contribute something to the cause. This group developed a list of every underwriting paradigm that ever existed—so extensive that no home would qualify for insurance. A three-member task force could have done a much better job—less expensively and more effectively.

On dozens of occasions, I have served on such committees for community organizations, our church, or an industry group. You've experienced this too. There are 50 people sitting there, all going along with the wishes of one strong person. If anyone disagrees with the direction, there is reluctance to speak out because "I must be the only one who disagrees." If I disagreed (which I often did), I would look around the room at the other 49 who seem to be happy with the direction being taken and ask myself, "Do I want to take on the other 49 and try to persuade them to my way of thinking?"

That's the "there's no skin off my nose" theory. If I dislike what's going on strongly enough, I can stop paying my dues, or my pledge, or take my membership elsewhere.

Why stir up friends and neighbors about something I can solve in another way?

We solved our IT problem by trimming down the 20 or 30 committee members to a three to five member team. Those three to five people represent the views of their departments. Each person is charged with the responsibility of making certain the interests of his or her department are being served. This representative is to keep the department manager informed of all the details of the project. If something goes wrong, the team member's neck is on the line. And if the project goes smoothly and is effective, that person gets credit and is recognized for it.

A team of four or five people, representing four or five affected departments (and two or three are even better) can get the job done—accurately and fast—while 20 or 30 see the project as a social activity. In the unlikely event the job is ever completed, chances are nobody will be happy with it.

Don't let anybody sell you on project teams of more than five or six people. The key is accountability. Lots of accountability.

SILVER BULLETS

▲ Committees are helpful with regard to communication, but they're seldom helpful for making decisions or getting things done.

▲ Call them teams, not committees. The term team has a connotation of action and results.

▲ A team of four or five people (two or three are even better) representing four or five affected departments can get the job done—accurately and faster—while 20 or 30 see the project as a social activity.

What's Next?

58
PREDICTING THE FUTURE

In ten years, will there be fewer companies or more companies competing in your field? Will profit margins be squeezed more or less? Will consumers demand better service or worse service? Will automation play a more important or less important role in your company?

Regardless of the industry, most leaders are in agreement that: there will continue to be consolidation in virtually every industry; it will be harder for any company to survive because profit margins will narrow; consumers will demand virtually instant service; and automation demands will be overwhelming as computers play a greater role in just about any business.

Any one of us could come up with a dozen similar questions—and we would agree on the answers, because the same trends are apparent in virtually any industry.

It's easy to predict the future. The hard part is to figure out what to do about it.

One thing is clear: If any business stands still, it will be run over.

The answer? Great leaders keep on learning. Forever. What's the best way to learn? Read.

Read several newspapers and business magazines. Watch for trends in any business. If you read two or three articles about a new trend emerging in, say, fast food, auto sales, women's clothing, anything, bisect it, dice it, and slice it. There just may be a message there that applies to your business. This is the way great leaders stay ahead of the competition.

Read biographies and autobiographies of business leaders. You'll read some good books and some bad books; you'll see some good management strategies and some bad management strategies, but you can learn from both the successes and the failures.

Many believe that the American education system is failing. I don't see that based on the young people we hire. The major weakness I see is that young people don't take time to read. They too often get their news from 15-second sound bites on TV. In ten or 15 seconds, I can learn all I want or need to learn about the murders, rapes, and fires that occurred last night. But to understand what's happening in our world in depth—to understand what's happening in the economy—to understand what's happening in business—it's necessary to read. I have found that the preponderance of our people do not have an in depth understanding of the one or two major news events outlined on the front page of today's newspaper unless it's scandal-related.

In our home, we have a little device that sifts out the junk on television and provides a lot more time to read. It's called an on/off switch. I would recommend that you look for that device, which I'm told is standard equipment on most TV sets, and give the off position a try. Once you start doing that regularly, you'll like it.

Yes, I know. Between little league baseball and soccer, dance lessons, music lessons, and forty other things in which the kids are involved, "we don't even have time to have dinner together, never mind time to read." May I suggest that you sit down as a family, establish priorities together—figure out what's really important in your lives—and carve out reading time in your daily schedules.

Reading . . . Learning. There is no better way to build a family—and no better way to build a business. There's seldom a need to reinvent the wheel. Others around us are inventing new wheels all the time. All we need to do is learn from them and apply what we learn.

SILVER BULLETS

▲ Great leaders keep on learning—and reading is the best way to learn.

▲ Read several newspapers and business magazines. Watch for trends in any business that may apply to your business.

▲ Read biographies and autobiographies of business leaders. You'll see good and bad management strategies, and you can learn from both.

▲ There's seldom a need to reinvent the wheel. Others around us are inventing new wheels all the time. All we need to do is learn from them and apply what we learn.

59

WHAT KEEPS YOU UP AT NIGHT?

In question and answer sessions following my last two speeches, members of my audiences asked, "What keeps you awake at nights?" I must have looked tired.

Outside of coffee with caffeine, not much. I have great confidence that the people in my company have the wherewithal to solve nearly any problem. I have confidence that they can compete with the toughest of competitors. I have confidence that they have the self-discipline to control expenses and keep them in line with sales. I have confidence that they have the self-discipline to price responsibly, yet competitively, regardless of what competitors might do. I have confidence that they will provide overwhelming service to our customers. With confidence like this, there's little need to lose sleep at night.

With good leadership, your company too can survive and prosper through the most difficult economic times, while battling with the fiercest of competitors.

But even with great leadership, there's one thing to worry about—not that it should keep you up nights—but you should certainly be concerned about it. *The free enterprise system must remain healthy.* Great companies can compete with the best of competitors. But even great companies cannot compete with government.

Remember the so-called 1990 luxury tax on boats priced at over $100,000? It seems that rich people needed boats a lot less than employees who build boats needed jobs. They stopped buying, and dozens of boat companies went out of business.

More recently, the California electric companies have had economic problems, primarily because of governmental bungling. One important factor was that wholesale prices of electricity were deregulated but retail prices were capped. No company can exist with such restraints for very long.

History is filled with similar examples. Taxes were imposed on glass in England in 1745. So glass manufacturers moved to Ireland. In 1796 a new tax was levied on windows, and that tax was increased ten times over the next 50 years. Why? Because windows in houses were symbols of the rich. So people started bricking up all but one or two windows in their homes. The glass tax was repealed in 1845.

There are rent controls in 150 cities in our country, creating jungles of slum lords—people who won't fix broken windows or hot water heaters to encourage tenants to move so that they can increase rents.

In my industry—property and casualty insurance—many price freezes and rate rollbacks have been dictated by legislators, while underlying costs for auto and home repairs, medical bills, law suits, and legal bills have kept rising. There are excess-profits laws calling for "negative profits" (I always called that a loss).

Banks are often required to lend money to people without regard to their ability to repay. Telephone, gas, and electric companies are required to continue services to indigent customers who never intend to pay for those services. There are caps on fees for taxi operators, and government dictates on services of cable companies. In one state, to obtain a permit to open a business, many months and thousands of dollars must be expended dealing with 72 government agencies.

I could go on. There are literally thousands of such situations—right here in America.

What could keep any of us awake at night? *This could happen in your industry*.

But there's something you can do about it: Always defend every aspect of the free enterprise system. Right now we don't do a very good job of that. You see, even great leaders often go unheard in this society because they are working 70 or 80 hours a week to meet payroll and make their businesses successful. They don't have time to posture for the TV camera (though it's not their nature to do so anyway). They just keep their heads down, work their tails off, and pay their taxes, while the politicians bash them and their businesses.

Most business people I talk to have become cynical about our nation's politicians, and for good reason. Yet our system of government is the best in the world, so we have to make it work better—and we *can* have influence.

A few years ago, we learned at the last minute that the Kentucky House of Representatives had voted to roll back auto insurance rates and to freeze them at the lower level for five years. That same bill was to be voted on by the State Senate that very day. Passage of the bill would have devastated the auto insurance market in that state. Our company for one would no longer have been able to provide auto insurance in Kentucky. We spent the day on the phone. Our people called every agent. We asked each one to call his or her state senator, and we outlined the message to deliver.

I spent most of my day calling our competitors, asking that they too call their agents. Many said, "There's nothing we can do," but others did make calls—and the bill was defeated in the Senate by one vote.

If a legislator receives 50 letters on a given issue that appear to be spontaneous and not an organized effort of a special interest group, he or she believes there is a groundswell of public opinion. We *can* have an impact on unfavorable legislation.

A number of years ago Sylvia and I had an opportunity to travel to China where I wrote down the guiding principles of the Chinese Communist Party:

1. Sufficient food

2. Adequate clothing

3. Basic shelter

4. Secure retirement

5. Decent burial

I don't know how they define *sufficient, adequate, secure,* and *decent,* but they don't mean what you and I think they mean in this country. No doubt about it, we live in the finest country in the world.

But we have a job to do. Business people have to get more involved in government. Much more involved. We must get personally acquainted with our legislators on a state and federal basis. When they don't support our views, we have to let them know. If they don't listen, we have to select different ones who will support free enterprise. Yes, this will cost us a few bucks each year (it seems the election cycles never stop), but it may be one of the best investments we can make to keep our businesses healthy. We can't rely on our trade associations and chambers of commerce to do it for us. *We* have to do it.

It's nearly bedtime as this chapter is being completed, and the issue has me stirred up. I'm afraid it will keep me awake tonight. I think I'll write my congressman.

SILVER BULLETS

▲ Good leadership will help your company survive and prosper through difficult economic times and through the fiercest of competition.

▲ Long-term survival requires that the free enterprise system remain healthy.

▲ History is filled with examples of private businesses being damaged severely or put out of business entirely by legislative dictates.

▲ Yet our system of government is the best in the world. We just have to find a way to make it work better.

▲ Business people must get more involved with government: become personally acquainted with legislators; help select candidates who will support free enterprise; and make contributions to their campaigns.

60

MAKING THE TRANSITION

Making a transition to a new senior management team is not easy. Yet, outside of raising a
family, nothing is more important.

The job really begins the day you assume a
new management assignment. You're looking
for a team that can get results—within the
philosophical framework we discussed. In
most cases you'll have to build that team—
strengthen some team members, bring others
into new management roles.

Your successor should be somewhere in that
mix. Or at least a *potential* successor should be
there.

Now, don't go out and tell this person far in
advance that he or she will be your successor,
because the odds are ten to one that you'll
change your mind before the time comes to
select a successor—probably more than once.
Sometimes your initial judgment is just plain

wrong. And almost certainly there will be a top performer whose performance drops suddenly—nearly overnight. It can result from alcohol problems, domestic problems, or health problems. The person you would have bet your next paycheck on becomes a washout, or at least becomes sidetracked while problems are getting worked out. I've seen this happen dozens of times.

The idea is to build and develop, build and develop, build and develop several people who may be up to the task when the time comes. Competition among them is healthy as long as it does not involve political backstabbing or other tactics that are damaging to the company.

If we've done our jobs well, we should have several possibilities from which to choose when retirement comes.

Of course, in many instances the decision of selecting a successor rests with a board committee. When reviewing candidates for my successor, I told our board committee, "If you like the performance of the company—if you like the direction we're going—here's the person you should select. If you don't like what has been going on here, don't select him. Go to the outside and look for another candidate."

Fortunately, our board followed my recommendations and selected the inside candidate who had been prepared for the job over a long period of time. He understood our business, he understood our philosophy of operation, and he understood our direction. He was our best communicator (an ingredient essential to leadership—you may have heard that before). Since he assumed the primary leadership role, company performance has remained near the top in our industry. The board committee did not make a mistake.

Our transition program had been successful.

SILVER BULLETS

▲ Making a transition to a new senior management team begins the day you assume a new management assignment.

▲ Don't tell a person far in advance that he or she will be your successor. Chances are you'll change you mind—probably more than once.

▲ Build and develop several people who may be up to the task when the time comes. At retirement time, there should be one, two, or three potential candidates.

61

THE TOOTH FAIRY'S FIRST RULE OF RETIREMENT

To cut through to the bottom line, this is a pitch for mandatory retirement policies. I support the idea strongly, despite the fact that retirement was one of the most painful periods of my life, along with admitting my father to a nursing home and going to my parents' funerals.

Yet, I've found that there's another life. I am nearing completion of my first book (this one) and have already started my second. An outline for the third has been completed.

My public speaking schedule is intensifying, and, well—this new life is not half-bad.

Some people are not ready to retire at age 65. Many are talented, aggressive thinkers with tremendous amounts of business experience that can add immeasurable value to business organizations. Others are ready to retire at 55 (if they have enough mental and physical challenges to keep them stimulated during their post-retirement years).

Certainly there are pros and cons, but I believe that a requirement for mandatory retirement at age 65 (for those to whom such a rule can apply under applicable state and federal laws) generally contributes to the health and welfare of most businesses.

Here's why. By the time those of us in CEO positions approach retirement years, generally we have shaped the company the way we want it to look. It's finally organized the way we want. The staff is in place to do things our way. And, in many cases, we are finally in a position to live the lifestyle we've always wanted—to work the hours we've always wanted.

I know a number of CEOs who still run their companies in the winter from their condos in Florida or Hawaii. "I have a phone, e-mail, a fax machine," they say. "I can do everything there that I can here." Wrong. Communication, the foundation of all leadership, is more than phone calls, e-mail, and fax machines. I call these folks e-mail managers (and that term doesn't just apply to those semi-retired). With e-mail, phone calls, and faxes, a manager can know exactly what others want him or her to know—with the facts spun the way others want them spun. But there's no remote control device on leadership. Leaders need to be there.

These CEOs have adopted the Tooth Fairy's First Rule of Retirement—never retire with a partial paycheck when you can retire with a full paycheck.

I don't know that anyone ever *intends* to do that. In most cases it creeps up on us. We may become a bit complacent. Perhaps a bit lazy. We may not do the necessary homework to stay abreast of industry changes, economic changes, and changes in customer demands.

The absence of a retirement policy makes it impossible to perpetuate management. I have seen companies with a 65-year-old CEO and an outstanding 45 year old COO who is the one who really makes the place tick. The 45 year old becomes discouraged and retires at 60 or 62, when the CEO is 80 or 82, leaving the company "high and dry" with no replacement in sight. Candidates for the job are fearful that the same thing will happen again, thinking the CEO might stay for another ten years.

With mandatory retirement policies in place, CEOs are under a little more pressure to perpetuate the management of the business. There's a sort of deadline—new management must be groomed and developed.

Again, I'm not suggesting that retirees be put out to pasture. There really are other lives out there—like writing books, consulting with other businesses, starting a new business, doing volunteer work, or getting a job with another company.

"What am I going to do?" one retiree asked when I suggested that he work until he dies. "Be a greeter at Wal-Mart?"

"I'd rather be a greeter at Wal-Mart," I answered, "than do nothing."

The human being is made to be physically and mentally challenged—clear to the end. And there are physical and mental challenges waiting out there for us. There's never a need for the Tooth Fairy's First Rule of Retirement.

SILVER BULLETS

▲ Mandatory retirement at 65 (when permitted by law) generally contributes to the health and welfare of most businesses.

▲ Some CEOs at age 65 become a bit complacent—perhaps a bit lazy—or do not do the necessary homework to stay abreast of industry and economic changes.

▲ The absence of a retirement policy makes it impossible to perpetuate management.

▲ It's not necessary that retirees be put out to pasture. There are other lives out there.

62
P.S.

Some things I almost forgot to tell you:

Show me a company that has a planning department and I'll show you a company that doesn't plan. Planning is an integral role of the leader. It can't be delegated to an outside department.

* * * * *

Nearly any problem becomes manageable when broken down into small parts. Be a dicer and slicer.

* * * * *

Have worthwhile goals. Companies shouldn't celebrate when they "beat plan," if the plan was to lose four cents on the dollar. That's like a football team celebrating a loss by two touchdowns because the other team was predicted to win by three touchdowns.

* * * * *

Adopt a JIT (Just In Time) training plan. Training that is done too early is lost before the new procedure goes into effect. Trainees need to be able to return to their desks and put the training to use immediately.

* * * * *

If you have questions, concerns, additions or corrections to anything I've expressed in this book, please e-mail me at rlbailey@dragonbbs.com. I'm still learning, and I would appreciate your comments.

Index

ACKNOWLEDGMENTS

This was the last segment of this book to be written, and it was the most difficult to write. Just where does one start when considering the names of those who have contributed to a lifetime of learning about business and leadership.

Heading the list must be the senior management team of the State Auto Insurance Companies, and especially Bob Moone, President, Chairman, and CEO (my successor at State Auto), Steve Johnston, Senior Vice President and Chief Financial Officer, and John Lowther, Senior Vice President, Secretary and General Counsel. These guys are good—and more than once they've pulled my tail out of the fire and kept me from making horrendous leadership mistakes.

Jim Dooley, State Auto's training manager, suggested that we add the *Silver Bullets* that summarize each chapter's key points.

Carolyn McBride, my assistant for many years, made sure I was where I was supposed to be when I was supposed to be there and otherwise made my work life relatively painless. In my new life as an unemployed senior citizen (i.e., author and public speaker), I still find myself yelling, "Carolyn, will you get . . ." when I realize that she's no longer here to help me. Gee, Carolyn, I miss you.

I wish I could name individually the some 1,300 members of the State Auto team. What a winning team it is! They made my job as their leader fun and rewarding.

Over my 43-year insurance career, I've had many bosses, and I learned from all of them. But I especially learned from two—Tom Mayhew and Paul Gingher.

As this book was nearing completion, I started to test the market a bit. "Is anyone really interested in still another book on leadership?" I asked myself. Franklin University Press, which focuses exclusively on leadership topics, was quick to see its value and gave me immediate encouragement. Dr. Paul Otte, President of Franklin University, kept pressing me for that first draft, offered a number of suggestions for its improvement, and kept reading the revised drafts when they were completed. When it was noted by our publisher that there should be something in the book about the author, Dr. Otte agreed to write it.

Dr. Stephen McClellan, director of Franklin University Press, got behind the project with youthful vigor and soon convinced me that this really is a darn good book—a very needed ingredient once weariness sets in after umpteen rewrites. He has kept us on schedule and has involved some exceptionally talented people who have helped us turn out a quality product. Joni Bentz Seal, Kelli Nowlin, Sean Hughes, and Kristina Givens should be singled out for special praise.

Dr. Martha Rogers, co-author of several best sellers (*The One to One Manager, The One to One Future, Enterprise One to One, One to One B2B*), honored me by offering to write the Foreword. I have the greatest respect for Dr. Rogers and her company, the Peppers and Rogers Group, the world's preeminent customer relationship management consulting and training firm.

And when Dr. Stephen R. Covey, the world-famous author of *The Seven Habits of Highly Effective People* (12,000,000 copies sold and translated into 32 languages), offered to endorse **PLAIN TALK ABOUT LEADERSHIP**, we were overwhelmed.

When it was time to consider artwork for the dust jacket, the publisher permitted me to seek the input of Nancy Elliott, one of the finest artists I know. For many years, Nancy was the graphic arts manager at State Auto. She and Bill Barnes of Robin Enterprises Co. were able to turn a not-well-explained idea into what I think is a pretty snazzy cover.

I can't imagine the number of times I've reread and revised chapters of this book. I still reread a chapter and say to myself, "I should have written this in another way." Or, "Here's another great story I should have included." But the deadline is approaching, so those stories will have to wait for subsequent books to follow soon.

The one segment I would most like to think about for a few more weeks is this Acknowledgments section. There are several people, I'm certain, whose names I have overlooked. To each and every one of you, I apologize. I will make it up to you as my dream is realized and other books are produced.

Finally, thanks to you, the readers, for investing your time and money in an effort to improve your leadership skills. My wish is that you will find this book to be an investment that will produce great dividends for your career and will help you build an overwhelmingly successful company. Godspeed.